BEVERLY ANDERSON

# Learning with LOGO

## Some classroom experiences

Cover taken from the original coloured frieze entitled TURTLELAND.

This was produced by children in the fourth year of St John's School, Digswell, Hertfordshire.

Teacher: Katrina Blythe.

Pupils: Alex, Anders, Andrew, Anne, Ben, Catherine, Chris, David, Dawn, Debbie, Frances, Joanna, Jonathan, Kathryn, Kerry G, Kerry M, Leighton, Matthew, Michele, Nicholas, Paul, Rachel, Robert, Rosemary, Ruth, Sarah Ed, Sarah El, Stephen, Tony.

© CET copyright, 1986

Microelectronics Education Programme

Printed by Riverside Press, Thanet Way, Whitstable, Kent.

## SPONSORS

MEP is most grateful to Acorn Computers Ltd, Logotron Ltd and AB European Marketing who have sponsored the printing of this book.

**Acorn Computers Ltd**
**Cambridge Technopark**
**645 Newmarket Road**
**Cambridge**
**CB5 8PD**
**Tel: 0223 214411**

# LOGOTRON

**Logotron Ltd**
**5 Granby Street**
**Loughborough**
**LE11 3DU**
**Tel: 0509 230248**

**AB European Marketing**
**Forest Farm Industrial Estate**
**Whitchurch**
**Cardiff**
**CF4 7YS**
**Tel: 0222 618336**

For information on products from these companies please use the order forms accompanying this book or write to the above addresses.

## Photographic credits

MEP acknowledges the help of the following companies and organisations in providing the photographs and illustrations for this book:

**Acorn Computers Ltd**

**Chiltern LOGO Project**

**Logotron Ltd**

**Sally and Richard Greenhill** — Photo Library: 01-607 8549 (pages 10, 11, 114, 130, 140, 155 and 170).

**Thames Television**

**Videotext Educational Publishing** (The illustrations that appear with a screen frame are taken off the MEP video *Turning Point:* see *Some useful resources* on page 188 for availability.)

**Walsall LOGO Project.**

# Contents

## STATE OF THE ART

## HEADTEACHERS TALKING

## COMMENTS AND CONCLUSIONS

# ACKNOWLEDGEMENTS

Though individual contributions and comments are acknowledged as they occur in the book, I would like to express my gratitude to the following for their help, forbearance and support:

The headteachers, staff and pupils of Green Close School, Delves Junior School and Hillary Junior School, all in Walsall; and of Marlborough School, Coleridge Road Infants School and Ickleford Primary School, all part of the Chiltern LOGO Project.

Warm thanks are due to Stephanie Orford, the staff and pupils of Greenwood House Assessment Centre; the headteacher and staff of Omagh Academy, and Ballyboley School, all in Northern Ireland; and to Margaret Murphy and Gray Horner of The Computer Centre at Stranmillis College, Belfast.

Others whose help has been invaluable include Ingrid Brindle, headteacher of Godley Primary School, Tameside; Richard Noss, Richard Bignell and Katrina Blythe of the Chiltern LOGO Project; Reg Ayres of St Paul and St Mary's College, Cheltenham; Julian Pixton and Linda Spear of the Walsall LOGO Project; Joe Johnson and David Walton from the Oxfordshire Education Authority. Derek Radburn, Chairman of the British LOGO Users' Group; Anita Straker and Christopher Schenk of the Microelectronics Education Programme (MEP) National Primary Project; Fran Colley and Bob Windsor who helped prepare the book for publication; and in particular Richard Fothergill, the Director of MEP, whose idea this book was.

All have put up with my ignorant questions and omnipresent tape recorder, and many have provided not only essential cups of staffroom tea, but best of all, the chance to share again in the joys of British primary school life.

The mistakes are mine but the work is theirs.

To obtain further copies of this book please contact:
**Tecmedia Limited, 5 Granby Street, Loughborough, LE11 3DU.
Telephone: 0509 230248.**

# FOREWORD

It is often difficult to identify events in education that create new
enthusiasms among teachers, but there is little doubt that the appear-
ance of Seymour Papert's book *Mindstorms: Children, Computers and
Powerful Ideas* initiated a great interest in the computer language LOGO.
Conferences followed quickly and have continued, and the enthusiasts
produced papers and gave speeches wherever they could. Some of
these were very theoretical, describing eloquently what could happen in
a classroom with the appropriate equipment. Some were the teachers
who first caught the enthusiasm and could see successful applications
occurring before them. Others talked about practice they had seen in
schools overseas, particularly in America, but many in the audience were
dubious about how relevant those experiences were in this country. In
addition, there was a Horizon film on the subject, almost entirely based
on American evidence, and the enthusiasts formed an association, the
British LOGO Users' Group.

One response from MEP was to form a project, based in the Chiltern
Region, which examined the learning activities being experienced by
children taught by the enthusiasts, and drew from these guidance, advice
and examples concerning the potential of the language. Another project
supported the development of working materials to help teachers, and
this work was undertaken in association with the Walsall Local Education
Authority. Finally, inservice training materials were prepared by our
Primary Project in Winchester, which formed the basis of courses
presented by advisers and tutors around the country.

However, it was felt that all this work was being undertaken and
promoted by the enthusiasts. Other questions remained unanswered. In
particular, we were curious to see how the practices associated with the
use of LOGO related to the excellent traditional work of teachers in
primary schools. What were the links to the present curriculum and did
LOGO enhance, expand or enlarge the experiences of children in the
general primary school or was it merely an interesting use of the microcomputer? What were the benefits seen by the ordinary (as opposed to
the enthusiast) teacher and their children? Were there many new and
different ways in which the language was being exploited?

To address these questions, MEP asked Beverly Anderson, an experienced and widely-respected primary teacher, to visit as many schools as she felt necessary to find out for us. She had no computer expertise, and that was an asset as we were interested in the learning and child development, not technicalities. Also she was sceptical, and that too was an advantage in getting a more balanced view. This book is the result of those visits and the analysis that Beverly made of what she saw. Beautifully written, it puts the impact of LOGO in its proper place, in the learning curriculum of children. This is not a research report, but rather a comprehensive case study, illuminated by the insight of an excellent teacher, giving a fair and balanced perception of the value and use of LOGO as it is currently practised in our primary schools.

Richard Fothergill
*Director*

*Microelectronics Education Programme*

February 1986

*Beverly Anderson*

# PREFACE

If you are a primary school teacher who knows nothing or very little about LOGO then this book is for you.

In the spring of 1983 I too had never heard of LOGO nor had I ever used a computer with a class of children. In addition, my background as a history and politics graduate is far from mathematical and it is only after years of helping infants that I have come to be fluent at addition and subtraction.

After more than 17 years in primary schools using a child-centred approach to learning and working chiefly through an integrated day, I can understand why conscientious teachers might be wary of suggestions that they add yet another element to an already overflowing curriculum.

But, as the use of computers becomes more widespread, it is imperative for teachers to come to terms with them and help their pupils to use them sensibly.

In 1982, I took part in an inservice Microelectronics Education Programme (MEP) video which reported on some interesting uses of computer programs in primary schools such as word processing, adventure games and data handling. I was intrigued by what I saw and, therefore, happily accepted the commission for a brief survey of what some children and their teachers were doing with LOGO and report on it for the benefit of teachers like myself who had yet to take the plunge.

What follows is very much a first look by a sceptical outsider. The time set for the task was unavoidably short and this is by no means a comprehensive survey of work with LOGO in British primary schools.

In the early stages of my investigations I visited Northern Ireland where I was able to see some of the work which is going on in a variety of schools there. I also spoke to enthusiastic teachers and advisers in Scotland, Wales and in several parts of England which I was unable to visit in person. I quickly realised that there is a lot of excellent work taking place in special education as well as in a number of primary schools and associated training colleges across the country.

In the end it seemed most sensible to look thoroughly at just a few schools which could offer between them a cross-section of activity, from the most tentative beginnings to quite sophisticated practice, and which included children from nursery school age up to twelve plus. I settled on some of the schools which were involved in the Chiltern and Walsall LOGO Projects and paid a number of visits to several classes within them.

I am very aware that this has meant ignoring outstanding work elsewhere and I hope that the schools and areas which have not been included will be the focus of future studies.

As several versions of LOGO have recently become available for the BBC microcomputer it is likely that the majority of teachers will soon be able to make use of LOGO's facilities. I hope that this set of case studies will be helpful to them in that process.

Beverly Anderson

February 1986

# An introduction

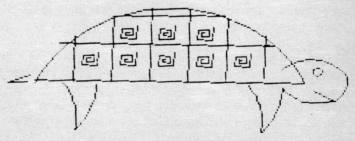

*See page 192 for the program to produce this Turtle.*

# 1 WHAT IS LOGO?

LOGO is a computer language which was specifically devised to make it easy for young children to create their own computer programs.

It was invented by Dr Seymour Papert and a team of American computer scientists, based at the Artificial Intelligence Laboratory of the Massachusetts Institute of Technology (MIT) in Boston.

The philosophy which gave rise to LOGO is explained by Dr Papert in his celebrated book *Mindstorms: Children, Computers and Powerful Ideas*. It is a fascinating book, well worth reading for its provocative ideas and the lively and humane intelligence of its author. In it Papert sets out his philosophy of education and his reasons for believing that computers can be an invaluable tool for encouraging child-centred learning.

Some of the ideas in *Mindstorms* fall outside the scope of this report, but others need to be described in some detail as they explain the principles behind LOGO and are relevant to its use in primary schools.

## Seymour Papert and Jean Piaget

Seymour Papert was born and educated in South Africa. In the foreword to *Mindstorms* he explains how as a two year old he 'fell in love' with motor cars and in particular with transmissions, gearboxes and differentials. He gradually came to understand how they worked and was able to use his knowledge of the principles behind them when he went to school and had to cope with such notions as multiplication tables and equations. This unusual experience may have had a bearing on his subsequent unorthodox conclusions about the nature and timing of what children learn.

In 1959, Papert went to Switzerland to work with Jean Piaget, the developmental psychologist, and spent five years at his Centre for Genetic Epistemology in Geneva.

Piaget was primarily interested in trying to identify the different stages through which a child's thinking passes as its mind develops. He showed, for instance, that at an early stage a child, confronted with the 'fact' that the same amount of water apparently takes up more space in tall, thin containers than in wide, shallow ones, will invent a personal explanation for this phenomenon which is not the true one. Piaget attributed this to the young child's inability to cope with abstract thought or what he called the stage of 'formal operations'.

Although Papert was profoundly influenced by Piaget he gradually became convinced that it is the culture in which a child grows which crucially influences the way the mind develops and on the order in which the Piagetian stages occur. 'What an individual can learn and how he learns it, depends on what models he has available.'

In his view the child's explanation for the liquid levels, for example, was perfectly logical. What made it inaccurate was the fact that the child had had less access to relevant experience than an adult. Any explanation founded on inadequate information would inevitably be inadequate. That did not necessarily mean that it was the result of immature thought.

## How computers can aid learning

In present-day cultures, he argues, children have many experiences early on in life which enable them to learn about such matters as one-to-one correspondence, counting on, and pairing. As he points out, many of the most important things in their daily lives, 'from socks to parents' tend to come in pairs. They also have numerous opportunites to build up an 'intuitive sense of quantity' by trying to decide, for example, whether to go for three large bits of chocolate or four smaller chunks.

To most teachers and parents this is commonplace. The fact that my nine year old son can, for instance, calculate very efficiently in sixties is probably due to the fact that he gets 60p pocket money every week. He can tell the time by the 24-hour digital display on his watch, but is not yet able to read an old-fashioned clock face despite several years of lessons at school.

Papert goes on to point out that what young children can't at present cope with is 'thinking about all the possible ways things could be, as opposed to the way they are'. After watching them learning to program computers while he was working with Piaget, he became convinced that the reason most children found some ideas difficult was not because their minds were not ready, as Piaget would have said, but because their experiences in a computer-starved culture were inadequate.

He uses as an example the finding that if most children under the age of eleven or twelve are presented with a set of coloured beads and asked to put down all the possible pairings such as red/blue, red/green, red/yellow and so on, then all the possible triple combinations, they find the problem impossible to work out. (Papert reminds us that some adults never manage to figure this out either!)

Two things are needed to work out an adequate solution, he says, and a child who is used to setting up a computer program will find the problem relatively simple. He calls the two techniques 'systematicity and debugging'.

The young programmer would find it natural to set up a system with two 'nested loops'. The first would select one colour and run all the other possible combinations against it; red/blue, red/green, red/yellow, red/black and so on. The second loop would repeat the exercise for each colour in turn; blue/green, blue/yellow, blue/black and so on. This sort of child would also be likely to spot and correct such 'bugs' or errors as double counting say the red/blue and blue/red combinations in the final list.

Papert's enthusiasm for computers as tools for learning is not confined to their value in helping children to think about mathematical ideas. If, as he believes, a particular kind of culture produces a certain pattern of learning development, then changing that culture is likely to alter the ways in which thinking develops. In his view this cultural change could most easily be brought about in a computer-rich society, which will be available to us soon.

## Children learn spontaneously

Papert is struck by the way in which a child learns spontaneously, when left to itself. He finds it attractive because all children do it, regardless of their ability, their learning costs nothing as it takes place without the help of schools or teachers, and the child enjoys it because the motivation is intrinsic, without the need for adult praise or punishment.

While working in Geneva with Piaget, Papert was struck by the way in which very young children learn left to themselves. He noticed the spontaneous and self-motivated manner in which early learning takes place and found it particularly attractive because it was common to all children, regardless of IQ, it was extremely cheap, taking place within the natural environment, and going on without the aid of schools or teachers. Babies and toddlers, in particular, learned naturally, for the joy of it, without the need for adult praise or punishment. Anyone who has watched a two year old working through the contents of a kitchen cupboard will know what Papert is referring to.

But in school even the best teaching, he says, forces children to listen to other people's explanations, especially about the mathematical aspects of knowledge, instead of allowing them the same freedom to find out for themselves that they have outside institutions.

The computer, he says, could be the key to overcoming this deficiency in present-day schooling and, properly used, can encourage a new way of learning. He calls it 'the Proteus of machines', potentially more influential than television or even the invention of printing. 'Its essence is its universality, its power to simulate. Because it can take on a thousand forms and can serve a thousand functions, it can appeal to a thousand tastes.' And the beauty of programming is that it allows the child to learn in an 'active and self-directed way'.

After several years with Piaget, to whose work he pays tribute, Papert decided that he wanted to find out how 'to create conditions for more knowledge to be acquired by children through the processes Piaget had identified'.

## Papert's move to MIT

In 1964 he moved to MIT, to work in the building which housed its artificial intelligence and computer science laboratories, and began what he called 'an experiment in cultural interaction'.

What would happen if computer scientists and children were brought together? From Piaget he had taken the notion that children teach themselves by building their own intellectual structures. But his own thinking emphasised 'two dimensions implicit but not elaborated in Piaget's own work: an interest in intellectual structures that could develop as opposed to those that actually at present do develop in the child, and the design of learning environments that are resonant with them'.

In other words, what would happen if children had access to computers in the way they now have access to pencils? Would they, as he believed, learn to use them in a 'masterful way' and in doing so change the way in which they learned everything else? Would they, by having access in a concrete way to some abstract ideas, be able to understand and use these ideas much sooner than Piaget would have thought likely?

In particular, as a mathematician and Piagetian psychologist he was keen to provide computer-based models which would help develop the thinking processes connected with moving in three dimensions, and problems connected with size and quantity. He rejected the traditional ways of teaching them as 'too deductive and knowledge based' as well as too static. Children, he thought, would benefit from having available a model that could move.

In addition he believed that if knowledge could be broken down into 'mind-sized chunks' children would find it easier to assimilate and use.

Papert hoped that children would be able to use computers as a vehicle for exploring abstract ideas in a concrete and personal way, which would be as powerful a model as the notion of gears had been for him. But for this to happen they would need access to computers with much better graphics and a far more flexible language than were available when he arrived at MIT.

## The creation of LOGO

So he set about creating a programming language and some ancillary devices which would make this possible and came up with LOGO and the Turtle.

LOGO was a new programming language, designed to be as powerful as the professional languages then in use but with 'easy entry routes for non-mathematical beginners'.

The name LOGO was chosen to emphasise the fact that this language was essentially based on symbols, not numbers, as is the case with a language like BASIC. To have confined children to programming in BASIC, Papert remarks, would have been like trying to teach poetry through translations in pidgin English.

Papert also invented a 'computer-controlled cybernetic animal' which he controlled by commands typed into a computer which had been programmed with LOGO.

There are two versions — a screen Turtle and a floor Turtle — both controlled by commands typed into a computer which has been programmed by LOGO.

Both types of Turtle have some important common features. Like humans, animals or cars, for instance, they have a front or heading. They also have a starting position and as they move from it they can leave a trace to show the path taken and the distance they have travelled. In these ways they satisfy Papert's desire to provide physical objects which can explore 'the mathematics of space and movement and repetitive patterns of action', which in his view come particularly naturally to children.

The Jessop floor Turtle is a mechanical object which can be picked up and moved about. Inside a transparent plastic housing sits a motor on wheels, so the whole contraption can move about on a floor, table top, or other flat surfaces. In the centre is a retractable tube which can take a felt-tipped pen. When the tube is extended the tip of the pen is flush with the ground and leaves a trace as the buggy moves.

Several versions of the floor Turtle are now available. Some are connected to the computer by a lead. One model, the Valiant Turtle, is powered by batteries and works by remote control, though it is still controlled from the computer. All the floor Turtles can be used to knock things over, like bulldozers or tanks, or to push objects along, such as balls, they can move around obstacles, up and down gradients, or act as pens.

*Floor Turtles — from left, the Jessop, the Zero 2 and the Valiant.*

The screen or light Turtle operates by the same principle as the floor
Turtle, but moves across a monitor screen instead of the classroom floor.
In some versions of LOGO, the screen Turtle is shaped like a triangle. In
other versions the Turtle resembles a tiny tortoise.

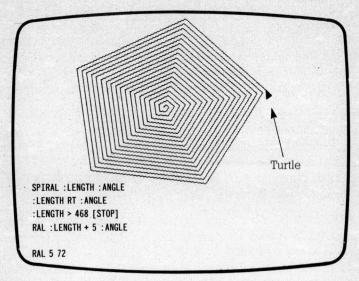

```
SPIRAL :LENGTH :ANGLE
:LENGTH RT :ANGLE
:LENGTH > 468 [STOP]
RAL :LENGTH + 5 :ANGLE

RAL 5 72
```

Turtle

*A screen Turtle, here shaped like a small triangle.*

Papert describes Turtles as 'abstract objects that live on computer
screens'. They share many of the important properties of the floor Turtle:
they move, they have a heading and they can obey commands. They
move more quickly than the eye can see and can be instructed to leave
a trace of brightly-coloured lines as they travel. In some cases, they can
be accompanied by sounds and music, shaped into little figures which
can then be animated or which can collide in a flash of explosive light.

Ideally, in his new learning environment Papert would prefer each child
to have free and constant access to an individual personal computer, just
as each now has a pencil. But even in today's more limited circumstances
he believes that a class with access to LOGO can create special
environments. These constitute 'artificially maintained oases where
people encounter knowledge (mathematical and mathetic) that has been
separated from the mainstream of the surrounding culture, indeed which
is even in some opposition to values expressed in that surrounding
culture'.

## Versions of LOGO

Versions of LOGO have been available for microcomputers such as the Commodore, Atari, Sinclair, Apple and RML machines for more than two years, and recently four versions have been produced for Acorn's BBC machines. There are also Turtle graphics packages called DART and ARROW which do not have all the features of the full LOGO. The differences will be referred to in a later chapter. Some versions of LOGO use slightly different spellings for the commands.

Each version of LOGO comes with a teacher's manual which explains how to use it. There are also a number of books available which describe LOGO and what to do with it. I found *LOGO: A Guide to Learning Through Programming* by Peter Goodyear (Ellis Horwood Ltd, Chichester and Heinemann Computers in Education Ltd, London, 1984) particularly helpful.

## Starting work with LOGO

To start work with LOGO a class needs a computer, a monitor and a version of LOGO suitable for that computer.

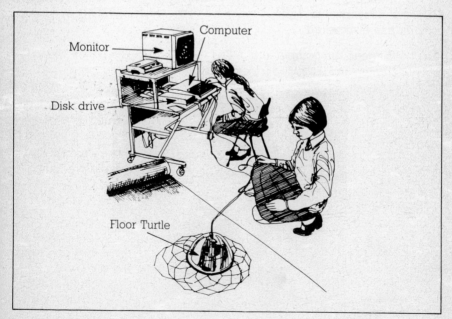

*Working with a floor Turtle.*

Some versions of LOGO are on a chip, others are on a disk, and some are in a ROM pack. If you are using a disk-based version of LOGO a disk drive is essential. If the version of LOGO is chip or pack-based, a disk drive is still highly desirable for storing work. Both a floor Turtle and a printer are optional extras but very useful.

Essentially what happens is as follows:

In order to get the floor Turtle to move around the child has to *talk* to it by typing instructions on the keyboard which activate the robot when the **RETURN** key is pressed.

If a simple instruction like **FORWARD 50** is typed in, then **RETURN**, the buggy rolls forward in a straight line in the direction it is facing for a distance of 50 of its units, then stops. **BACKWARD 50**, then **RETURN** would bring it back to its starting point.

**RIGHT 90**, then **RETURN** causes the front of the Turtle to move through 90°. It can then be programmed to move forward from this new heading, or left through the required number of degrees, or backwards.

**PENUP** means that the felt tip is retracted so that the Turtle moves without leaving a trace on the floor or paper. **PENDOWN** means that a permanent record of its journey is made, not always conveniently, as more than one teacher has discovered!

Any message to the computer is in fact a program, even if all it consists of is one command: **FORWARD 50**, then **RETURN**.

*The Zero 2 in PENDOWN position.*

Children can make the Turtle move by issuing instructions randomly. This is called *direct drive*. Instructions typed in can always be changed by pressing **DELETE** or **RUBOUT** before the **RETURN** key is pressed. When children want to save a program they can learn to put it into the computer's memory to be retrieved and reused.

The **REPEAT** facility allows them to issue an instruction, which is then repeated as many times as they say, so that, for example, a square can be drawn by instructing the Turtle to move **FORWARD 47 RIGHT 90** four times. Simple shapes can be drawn out repeatedly from slightly different starting points so that rows of squares or triangles can be drawn or hexagons can be traced out in a circular pattern to produce a flower-head pattern. A square can be drawn with a triangle on top to make a house, and so on.

By building up programs gradually the child is able to learn in Papert's 'mind-sized chunks'. But even more importantly, this sort of activity gives the child the upper hand at all times since the child is telling the computer what to do, not the other way around. Many computer programs require the child to follow instructions. Some programs are also designed to test a child. Papert's system gives the initiative to the child.

*Drawing a flower pattern with a screen Turtle.*

Once children begin to build programs using a screen Turtle they find it useful to have access to a printer as well, so that they can produce permanent *hard copy* (or paper) records of the work which they create on the screen.

## Learning how to use LOGO

Learning to program with LOGO benefits children in a number of ways, according to Papert. The ability to 'create programs that produce pleasing graphics, funny pictures, sound effects, music and computer jokes' gives children the satisfaction of using their mathematics inventively on activities connected to life outside school.

Flying a simulated spaceship or programming a sequence of street lights on a model, for example, allows them to learn through playful simulation which is connected to the working world of adults.

Since the problems are invented and solved by the children themselves, they and their teachers can learn together as partners without the need for a set curriculum.

*Debugging* is an essential and attractive feature of working with LOGO, though it is common to all computer programs. 'Finding a bug' means tracking down the reason why a program is failing to do what it has been told and rectifying the error.

Many LOGOs show that there is a bug in the child's program by flashing up such messages as **LOGO DOESN'T KNOW HOW TO** whatever it is, or **I DON'T KNOW HOW TO** ... thus making it clear that it is the computer which has failed to understand the child. This feature further reinforces the child's sense of power and control, which Papert regards as vitally important.

Since most attempts to build a computer program seldom work perfectly the first time around, he is convinced that by working with computers in this way children can be freed from the belief that learning involves being either right or wrong. As children become 'master programmers' they become adept at isolating and correcting bugs. They learn to ask, not whether the program is right or wrong, but 'if it is fixable'.

By rearranging or amending small items in a program children are allowed to 'tinker' with small bits of knowledge in a concrete way which Papert believes is particularly appropriate because it matches up to the way we all learn, left to ourselves.

The average person's natural way of thinking is 'chaotic and untidy' he says, yet it is perfectly possible to use powerful ideas while we are thinking in this fashion.

He describes natural thinking as a process whereby all sorts of skills and thinking strategies are thrown together into a sort of mental 'tool-box'.

Each act of learning may enter separately. But as the 'tools' jostle around together they may well affect and change each other, a notion which accords with Piaget's stages of accommodation and assimilation.

This 'tinkering with what you've got' is similar to the way children operate as they devise or debug their programs. But with LOGO children's learning does not have to remain abstract. As they learn, the bits of knowledge or ideas become concrete and they appear in front of their eyes, either in the form of listed sets of commands or drawn out on paper or screen through the medium of the Turtles.

## The benefits for mathematics education

LOGO has another important virtue, according to its creator. It can help break down what he calls a prevailing 'mathophobic bias' in education, which is painful to someone like Papert who has loved mathematics since childhood.

The reason so many people hate mathematics at school is, he says, because traditionally it has been taught in a 'mathetic way' which emphasises logical, coherent patterns of thinking.

This is particularly unfortunate, he believes, since true mathematics is, in fact, much more similar to natural ways of thinking than to the school version, so many people are being unnecessarily put off and depressed.

He believes too that traditional mathematics teaching cuts mathematics off artificially from other areas of learning such as language or movement, which use different modes of thinking.

There are three essential principles needed if mathematics is to be accessible:
1   It must be continuous with personal experience
2   It must empower the child to work at meaningful projects which could not be achieved without it
3   The topic the child engages in must have some relevance in the larger society or culture which the child shares with adults.

Working with LOGO, says its creator, will allow a child to experience all three crucial aspects of accessible mathematics.

Papert's overall aim in creating LOGO was not merely to provide a more attractive way into mathematics. His intention was to provide a tool which would encourage joyful and independent learning in young children.

## Are all of Papert's claims true?

At this point many experienced teachers may well be feeling restless. What, they might well ask, have we been doing in our classrooms all this time? After all, in British primary schools central importance is placed on promoting learning which is rooted in children's own knowledge and interests, and teachers often encourage their pupils to look upon mistakes as a valuable and creative part of learning. Such teachers might want to challenge some of Papert's claims for computer-based learning and particularly for LOGO.

Is there really no other way to encourage independent, systematic thought? Does LOGO indeed have some characteristics which make it uniquely valuable?

Papert does acknowledge that the learning strategies he describes pre-date the computer and are not unique to working with it. But he believes that 'thinking about learning by analogy with developing a program is a powerful and accessible way to get started on becoming more articulate about one's debugging strategies and more deliberate about improving them' and to a number of the British teachers who have worked with LOGO, this is indeed one of its most attractive features.

In the case studies and conversations which follow I have tried to describe some of the work going on in a few of the schools where teachers and children have been learning to use LOGO. I have started with a nursery class and end with twelve year olds at the top of a middle school. In addition, some headteachers talk about the general issues connected with getting LOGO going in a school.

I hope that these descriptions and conversations will help to provide some account of ways in which Papert's ideas are bearing fruit in British primary schools and that teachers who are unfamiliar with this kind of work will have some evidence on which to base their evaluation of its potential usefulness for themselves and the children they are helping to learn.

# Starting out

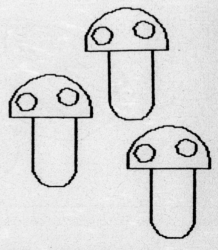

*See page 194 for the program to produce these toadstools.*

# 2 USING LOGO IN A NURSERY CLASS

The following case studies describe how some teachers of young children begin work with LOGO.

## What is Big Trak?

A number of schools make use of a Big Trak before introducing the floor Turtle. Big Trak is a toy tank which can be programmed and through it children can learn some of the basic words and procedures that they will need later for using a computer keyboard to control a floor Turtle.

*Big Trak (a programmable toy) showing an enlargement of its keyboard.*

The tank is mounted on large rubber wheels. On its back is a display consisting of numbered keys, each of which has a different purpose. The numbers from nought to nine drive the machine forward a certain distance, usually one or more times the length of the Big Trak. There are four direction keys — arrows pointing forwards, backwards, left and right. Typing CM clears the memory ready for a new program; CE cancels the previous instruction; P is the pause button, and when GO is pressed the Big Trak lurches forward, noisily grunting as it moves. When it stops it plays a little tune. It can be made to *fire* a series of shots by pressing the photon light button. X2 is a repeat key.

Big Trak is a beguiling toy and its value in preparing for LOGO work will be described later in this chapter. But first a look at the nursery class at Green Close School, Walsall.

## Using Big Trak in a nursery class

Green Close is a junior mixed and infant school in Walsall, West Midlands. It is about 50 years old and at present has about 300 children on roll. An infant and a junior class will be featured in later chapters.

The nursery contains three and four year olds. On the day I visited, the children were working in groups at the usual nursery activities, sand and water play, modelling, painting, driving model cars over a road lay-out, matching numbers at a table with the assistance of the classroom helper.

Mrs Corbett, the nursery nurse in charge of the class, was sitting in the carpeted area with a group of three children. She stood them up in turn on a large cardboard arrow, then moved them forward onto a blue cardboard rectangle. As the child moved she said the words 'forward' then 'arrow', which the child repeated.

This is a form of pre-Big Trak preparatory work, which accustoms the children to the idea of using the buttons in sequence and shows them what the commands will make Big Trak do, but it ties in with other activities like colour matching, shape or number matching.

For children who were ready for the second stage Mrs Corbett had set up cut-out models of three dogs, each with a bowl in front of it, coloured red, blue or yellow. In front of her, as she knelt on the carpet with two four year olds, was a bowl containing a number of coloured cardboard bones.

'The dogs are hungry. Shall we give them a bone each?' One child chose a yellow bone and took it to the correct dog.

'Which way do you have to go?' asked Mrs Corbett. 'That's right. Go forwards.'

The boy headed for the yellow dish and deposited his bone. This direction and colour-matching activity was repeated for the other two in the group.

At the next stage there was a row of three large cut-out house facades, each with a coloured front door with a cut-out slot in it for the letter box.

In front of the yellow door was a yellow rectangle equivalent to one Big Trak length, and a blue cardboard Big Trak outline. Beside these was a large blue arrow cut out in card.

The blue door had a blue strip in front of it as long as two Big Trak lengths plus the blue Big Trak outline, with two arrows alongside these shapes. The red door's strip was three Big Traks long, and it too started with a blue outline with the two arrows alongside.

The Big Trak keyboard had been concealed beneath an overlay which had a red dot over the number three, a blue dot over the two and yellow over the one. Big Trak was to be a postman delivering letters to the houses.

Each child selected a *letter* made of red, blue or yellow card. Big Trak was placed on to its blue card outline in front of the appropriately coloured front door. Then it was turned on.

The child cleared the memory, using the **CM** key, which had been left exposed through the overlay. They had learned to call this the *forget* key. The *forward* arrow, which had also been left exposed, was pressed, then the key which was the same colour as the chosen letter and matching front door. The coloured letter was put onto Big Trak's back then the **GO** button was pressed.

With a chortling grunt Big Trak set off noisily and arrived at the front door. The letter was posted through the letterbox.

## The value of Big Trak

Mrs Corbett told me that part of the value of using Big Trak in the nursery is the way that it encourages the development of language. 'As well as learning new words like **FORWARD**, when I ask them questions such as: Where is it going? Why is it doing that? they have to think and use new words to give a sensible reply. I also value the social skills that are developed out of having to take turns, for instance.'

She stressed that the things I had seen were not part of any set syllabus. Her approach is flexible and she adapts the games to the needs of the particular children in the group. The Big Trak activities are an integral part of her overall nursery class routine and fit comfortably into it.

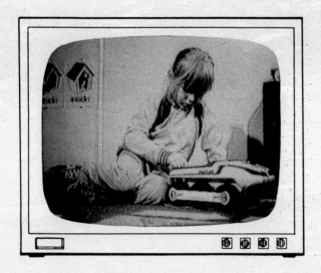

*Pressing the keys to program Big Trak.*

## 3 BEGINNING WITH THE FLOOR TURTLE

In some schools the infants are introduced to the floor Turtle without Big Trak first.

### Drawing a rocket in a top infant class

Ickleford Primary School is in a village to the north of London, near Hitchin in Hertfordshire.

A class of top infants was gathered on the carpet the day I arrived, watching one boy proudly programming a floor Turtle to draw out a rocket which he had designed. He had drawn it and planned the commands during free time while the rest of the class were doing puzzles or playing in the Wendy House, and this unusual solo performance was a special reward for the effort.

His teacher, Mrs Marion Harrison, had given him a hand. He had come to her with half a rocket drawn, then she had shown him how to make it symmetrical by matching the second half to his initial outline. He drew it out on to squared paper and called each square ten. By counting the squares he was able to write out the likely sequence of commands he would need to make the Turtle draw out the shape correctly.

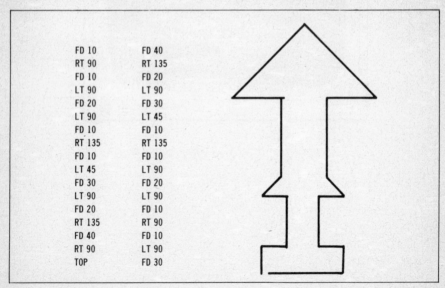

| | |
|---|---|
| FD 10 | FD 40 |
| RT 90 | RT 135 |
| FD 10 | FD 20 |
| LT 90 | LT 90 |
| FD 20 | FD 30 |
| LT 90 | LT 45 |
| FD 10 | FD 10 |
| RT 135 | RT 135 |
| FD 10 | FD 10 |
| LT 45 | LT 90 |
| FD 30 | FD 20 |
| LT 90 | LT 90 |
| FD 20 | FD 10 |
| RT 135 | RT 90 |
| FD 40 | FD 10 |
| RT 90 | LT 90 |
| TOP | FD 30 |

*These commands are shown as they were written on paper. On the right is the rocket shape drawn by the floor Turtle.*

The floor Turtle had been placed on a large piece of paper which was taped to the floor. The boy stood typing at a computer monitor and keyboard and as he typed in the commands he sounded out the letters phonetically: 'F-o-r-w-a-r-d 50 r-e-t-u-r-n'. Each time **RETURN** was pressed the floor Turtle moved, leaving a trace on the white card.

The boy showed me a sequence of commands (or a procedure) which consisted of a list of instructions such as **FORWARD 40 RIGHT 90 FORWARD 30** and so on. The version of LOGO used by this class allows the children to try out their procedure on the screen before instructing the floor Turtle to draw it out. If the drawing is not quite what they expected they can correct any flaws in the program before the Turtle actually draws out the shape on the board.

'I tried it out and it didn't work. When that (an item in the list of commands) said 60 it wasn't 60, so I tried 30.'

'That's right', said Mrs Harrison. 'For some reason 60 didn't quite close the gap at the bottom of the rocket. I noticed that he had written down some of the turns the wrong way round, left instead of right for instance, so they had to be changed. It was a good job we tested it first wasn't it? So then what did we decide to do?'

The boy answered, 'Type it all into the memory'.

'That took a long time didn't it? What did we have to type in between each command?'

'And.'

'Good. Now we've got it into the memory. What next? Oh, wait a minute. Is the pen up or pen down?'

'Down.'

'No, up, it's lifted up.' (Chorus of voices.)

'So, type in drop pen.'

'D-r-o-p . . .'

'Now what are you going to type in?'

'Rocket.'

'Right and it's here on the screen for you to see, isn't it?'

As the word rocket was already on the screen the boy used it as a spelling guide while he searched for the letters on the keyboard.

The Turtle drew out the rocket. There was an enthralled silence and then a burst of spontaneous applause from the rest of the class.

## Robots, flowers and a Weetabix lorry

Mrs Harrison remarked that since working with LOGO and having to deal with numbers over ten, more than one child who previously hadn't been able to count up to more than ten in class could now add, say, 20 to 30 with ease.

Some of the children told me what they had drawn with the floor Turtle, consulting notebooks in which their lists of procedures were kept.

'Me and Gary and Wayne made a robot, and now we've made a church. We still have to put in a few windows.'

'Stephanie and me made a carnation. We used four hexagons.'

Helen: 'We've made a flower and now we're doing a stalk. We had to do four hexagons for the petals then when we'd done it we decided we'd do a stalk so we just did a line. Then for two leaves at the bottom we did two more hexagons. Now we are working on a face.'

Stuart had made a robot and a Weetabix lorry:

'Well we made pentagon wheels for it then we made the truck, its actual body. Then we put a line across it so we could put the sign up. We only got 'weeta', we didn't get the 'ix' on it because we cut it off.

The Turtle is fun. If something goes wrong you call a teacher or else you press **ESCAPE**.

It's quite easy to correct mistakes. If we haven't done **RETURN** yet we usually press the **DELETE** button.'

Alexander said, 'I made a circle'.

I asked, 'How did you figure it out?'

'Well we knew that a whole turn was 360 so my friend said, 'Shall we try doing **REPEAT 360** times, **FD 1** and **RT 1**?' And it worked.'

Vanessa: 'I have made a triangle. It took a little time.'

And another child: 'I've made a bottle. It was a bit tricky but I drawed it out on a piece of squared paper then I worked out the constructions of it. Then we tested it on the computer and it worked but it went a little wrong so we had to make it a straw going into the bottle.'

Melissa talked about mistakes: 'Well if the pen's down and you just tell it to draw it, it will and you just have to make it into something else. If the pen is up you can press **DELETE** and it rubs it out on the screen.'

She also said: 'I like working with the computer because the thing that you make makes you very proud when you have drawn it.'

## Children's writing from a wall display

- We have got a computer with a Turtle and the Turtle can draw by typing commands and the computer is fun.

- I like the computer. I like the Turtle. The Turtle can make squares and rectangles.

- I like the computer because it draws a picture like out of a box and Ian and Michelle go on it with me. I helped her and I told the computer to do L100 for a square and then we did a square body for it and some arms.

- I like the computer but sometimes it is hard. I like the Turtle's face. First you put paper on the floor then you put the Turtle on and type a command. I like it when you save your procedures. On Tuesday Helen and I drew a carnation. Helen and I type in HEX RETURN and it'll draw a hexagon. We drew the carnation with four hexagons and a line for the stalk and a hexagon for leaves.

● I went on the computer today and I go on the computer with Emma and Kim and we did a dog first. I like going on the computer. We go on the computer on Thursdays. What day do you go on the computer? What do you draw? You can draw a bottle. I did. First I did the command on paper and I did it on the computer.

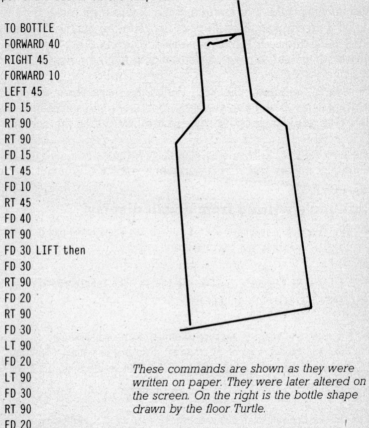

```
TO BOTTLE
FORWARD 40
RIGHT 45
FORWARD 10
LEFT 45
FD 15
RT 90
RT 90
FD 15
LT 45
FD 10
RT 45
FD 40
RT 90
FD 30 LIFT then
FD 30
RT 90
FD 20
RT 90
FD 30
LT 90
FD 20
LT 90
FD 30
RT 90
FD 20
```

*These commands are shown as they were written on paper. They were later altered on the screen. On the right is the bottle shape drawn by the floor Turtle.*

and it DID IT!!

Adam explained how LOGO works:

● We have got a computer at school and we call it Jessie and it draws things on paper. You have to give it commands and I like the computer because you would not have to do the whole word. You just have to do this — FD for forwards and BD for back and RT for right and LT for left and that's what I like about the computer.

And you can say this for a square – BUILD SQUARE REPEAT 4 FORWARDS 50 and LEFT 90 ESC for ESCAPE SQUARE and it would draw a square, and that is all the rest of what I like about the computer and I like the way he looks.

Adam is six.

Three boys did a project together called *The Iron Man*:

● On the computer me and Adam drew the Iron Man and we have saved the leg. Its size is 50 long and 10 wide and the square is 5 each edge. The foot is size 20 long and 10 wide. Sometimes I find it hard and sometimes I find it easy as well. You have to type in what you want it to do.

*The Iron Man drawn by the floor Turtle.*

# Starting work with the Turtle

At the time of my visit this class had only been working with the Turtle for four weeks. Although it was their first term already a wide range of skills had become apparent. The children making the eyes for the Iron Man's face, part of their large Iron Man picture, were saving procedures and understood what they were doing. The girls making the flower were working in direct drive, putting in instructions individually and experimentally, then pressing **RETURN** and watching what happened.

It was explained to me that not only were the boys working on the Iron Man able to put procedures together to make a face, but they also understood how to adapt the procedure they had already built for the face to draw the little curls down the side of the face, their next job.

*How had the class got started?*

Mrs Harrison explained:

'We started in September with what I call pre-Turtle work, moving forwards and backwards around the room. We talked a lot about degrees. Do you remember, children, when you had to get me from here to the other side of the room by giving me commands about how to move and you landed me up in the blackboard?

In fact, we did a lot of pre-Turtle work. The children and I took turns being the Turtle. We walked around the hall and classroom directing each other. We had a lot of work sheets because at this age they don't even know their right from their left, so they had to draw a man in the middle of the picture, draw something on his left-hand side, something on his right and so on.

We did that sort of activity for almost a term before we had the Turtle in the room and then, because they really knew about moving forward, backwards or turning, a lot of them were able to understand right angles. Some of them still call left angles right angles, though.

When I first brought the Turtle into the room I said to the children, 'How do you think it's going to work?' We had played at being the Turtle and issued voice control demands to it and so one little lad, full of ideas, put his hand up, stood up to his full height in front of the Turtle and said 'Forward one!'

Of course the Turtle didn't move. He said it louder and it still didn't work. Someone saw the keyboard and decided that might have something to do with it and then they were away.

After that it was just a matter of getting used to the keyboard. We had two or three sessions where I played with it and everybody watched, then a few people came out and had a go.

Some of these children are very competent and will find the letters easily. One little girl who doesn't recognise the letters of the alphabet consistently has a bit of trouble. She can barely draw a straight line because she makes so many typing errors, but the two little boys she's with help her a lot and point at the key she has to press next, so she's gaining something. She wants to learn her letters because she enjoys the computer and is eager to have her turn.'

*Do they plan or just try things out?*

'Both. When they have done their work for the day there are various activities that they can do for five or ten minutes. Everyone now has a computer folder and they can get it out and use some squared paper to work out what they would like to do when it's their turn on the computer. That's given one or two ideas.

At first they were a bit nervous or short of inspiration and tended just to draw a house or flat or square, but they are becoming more ambitious now. I also have some work cards on which I have drawn half the picture and they have to draw the other half. They copy that on to some paper. We tend to use squared paper so they can then call each square five Turtle units or ten.

I think there has been considerable improvement in maths. When they came to me in September as top infants the average child was really only familiar with numbers up to 20. So if you said to them 'Tell the Turtle to do a large number of units forwards', they'd answer 22.

We had to do a lot of counting in fives and tens because one Turtle unit is a hiccup. If you told the Turtle to move forward ten that would be about two centimetres I suppose.

Of course, to these children ten was a big number so they couldn't operate very well within those limits. We had to do a lot of work very rapidly on the numbers up to a hundred and place value before the computer arrived because I knew from last year's experience that it was needed.

Now the average child will type in 80 when I ask for a large number and they have a better idea of what it really means. At first the less able child homed in on 90 because of 90°, so they were moving forward 90 and back 90 as well as right 90. 'That's too far', I said. 'Let's have something smaller.'

'89?'

Now some children are more advanced in the use of high numbers than they would probably have been without the Turtle. The able ones can handle numbers over 100 quite well and I put more emphasis on counting to 100 and looking at the actual numbers.

That might not be appropriate with every top infant class, but because of my interest in computers we've done it. We count on and count back and so on. In many cases they can tell you that half of 360 is 180 and half of 180 is 90. They can handle it because the need is there.'

## From square wheels to round wheels

'One day a group came bouncing in after half-term to say they thought they knew how to do a circle. I don't know where they had got it from, but they were fed up with square wheels on their cars.

One said, 'If you moved lots of times forward one right one that would make a circle, wouldn't it?'

I said, 'I don't know, possibly. But how many times would you have to move altogether?'

They thought about it and one of them said 120 or 160, off the top of their head; this was in an afternoon talking time.

I asked, 'When you did the square how many right angles did you do?'

'Oh — four.'

'Well, what was each right angle?'

'That was 90. Ah! Four nineties, that was 360', they said because that was a complete turn.

They immediately thought that if they moved 360 times forward and right one it would give them a circle. So off they went to try it out and, of course, it worked. Absolutely priceless, you should have seen their faces. I wish I'd had a camera. The whole class was absolutely agog and amazed that it had worked.

Next day another group wanted to do a face, because this term we are doing a project about *My Five Senses*, looking at faces, eyes and ears. They said, 'Well we can look up the way the other group did it'. They were a little put out when I wouldn't let them use it.

I think they must work these things out for themselves, otherwise they are just copying and don't understand the maths work involved. That's pointless.

They could, after all, go to the computer procedure book we've got and copy all sorts of things, just typing them in. They're not learning that way.

If we wanted to produce a big picture quickly for the wall, as we've done in the past, I wouldn't mind them using each other's procedures, but while they are trying to learn — no. Mark you, I have noticed this year that they seem to have picked up the idea about 90° being a quarter turn without having to try it out for themselves, so they do get things from each other.'

## Some reflections and predictions

*How much experience had you had yourself before you started working with your class?*

'None, well almost none. I'd been on a course for two-and-a-half days but that was mainly with DART and commercial material and nothing worked at all because of technical foul-ups.

I picked it up by trial and error. I took the set-up home and played around at lunchtime. I think I'm just about half a step ahead of the children.'

*What do you think your children have got out of working with LOGO and the Turtle?*

'Their maths has improved, their estimating ability, which is linked to other sorts of school work. They're not so frightened of modern technology. And they have had fun.'

*Have they had trouble working in groups of threes, being so young?*

'Sometimes. I've had to reshuffle one or two groups because it's been obvious that some were taking the lead and one person was standing around doing nothing. At the moment they are pretty evenly matched so that if three quiet people are together one of them has got to take action! And if you have three argumentative people together they have to learn how to cope with taking turns.

One week one boy said he wanted to draw a lorry. The others said no, they were going to draw a car and there was almost a stand-up fight, but in the end they had to agree that they were going to draw the car because two people wanted to do that as against the one.'

*Where do most of their ideas come from?*

'Some of them are based on projects within the class, some are free ideas. I have noticed that the girls tend to draw houses. I suppose to begin with because a square was the easiest thing to draw and can easily turn into a house. The boys tend to go for robots and machines of some sort.

They don't find their mistakes frustrating, but what does upset them is when the machine doesn't work and they can't have their turn.'

*Where do you think they'll go next?*

'Different sized circles. I've told them in a talk that a circle must be 360°, so however many times they repeat multiplied by, the angle must be 360°. We talked about the squares and they've made an octagon and some triangles and they know that, but their mathematical ability isn't good enough yet to work it out.

It really is going to be trial and error. They will be able to keep the results of their experiments to refer to and I hope one day daylight will dawn or their maths ability will increase.

I know that the juniors use a calculator, but I don't think mine are ready for that yet.

I must admit that I had great reservations about starting this sort of work with LOGO because as far as I was concerned the three Rs were not going to suffer.

It takes a lot of organisation as to when each group can go to the computer, but I'd hate to be without it now, I really would.'

*Is there any advice you'd give to an infant teacher about to start Turtle work?*

'Yes. Take it slowly. Don't be worried if you yourself don't know very much, and don't try to push them on too fast. Just let the children experiment and have fun.'

# 4 A DIFFERENT START

Marilyn Metz used a slightly different approach with her top infants at Coleridge Road Infants School in North London. This class, a part of the Chiltern LOGO Project, was assisted by Richard Noss, then the Project coordinator, who sorted out hardware failures as well as giving advice about working with the Turtle.

This is the second year that Mrs Metz has used LOGO with a class of six to seven year olds. At present she has available an Apple II system, and two Commodore 64s, each of which runs a floor Turtle which she shares with the parallel class.

The Apple has an Epson printer attached which prints out every command the child types in, so it is possible to have a record of the children's experiments in direct drive every step of the way. In contrast, the Commodore printer dumps pictures and prints out finished procedures only.

Mrs Metz explained her approach:

'In September 1983 I started with a class of 25 children.

At that time I had an Apple, with Apple LOGO and a floor Turtle. I took a deep breath and gave them LOGO very early on in the year.

The introduction was fairly simple. I told them that we would be using a language called LOGO on a computer, and that they could use it to talk to a little machine called a floor Turtle, which drew pictures.'

## Learning LOGO is like learning English

'I made the analogy of LOGO being like English and since many of the children in my class speak more than one language they didn't find the idea of learning a new one difficult.

I explained that they would only need to learn a few words to start with, six simple commands — FORWARD, BACKWARD, LEFT, RIGHT, PENUP and PENDOWN. I also told them from the beginning that they could teach the Turtle to remember, so they had the idea that they could write procedures right from the start.

I explained about a disk being like a filing cabinet with lots of information inside. I said it was locked and you couldn't open it, but by teaching the Turtle to remember you were putting information into it. If you wanted a copy of what you had taught the Turtle, you asked for it by telling the computer to read your file into its memory.

Most of the children haven't used the space which is theirs, but I see no harm in giving them the technological framework right at the beginning, rather than waiting till the need arises.

I did very little preparatory work apart from making some flash cards which spelled out the commands and also gave a pictorial representation of them, such as an arrow pointing right for right. We went through several versions until I produced a set that they could understand. From time to time I found I had to remind them of how the system works, that they would have to read in their file and save it, general rules like that.

I don't give them any procedures. They control the Turtle in direct drive until they decide that they want to teach it to remember.

One of the things I hadn't foreseen was that not having a particular sort of printer to fall back on would force the children to see the need to make their own record.

Last year, because we had the printer, the children were very reluctant to record on paper or plan in advance because they knew that they could get a hard-copy print-out. This year, because the Commodore does not print out the full set of commands from the screen, they are quite keen to record. Some are even writing out commands on paper before they get to the system and then trying them out, which is quite sophisticated.

At first they worked in threes, but pretty quickly we found that pairs worked better. The amount of time each pair gets was left completely flexible at first, too flexible I think, in that some pairs were probably left to work on too long. A single-minded pair, which has a clear idea of what it wants to achieve, will probably find half-an-hour enough. Some children need to have time to warm up and they may need as much as three-quarters of an hour.

If someone is really involved I will allow them to carry on beyond that time until they have finished their task, but I keep a weather-eye on motivation and if they have come to a natural break, I stop them.'

# Different types of hardware

'It may be worth talking briefly about the different kinds of hardware. They all have different qualities and I find that the children get used to coping with the various characteristics in a matter-of-fact way.

The Apple system was set up so that the children's disks were automatically loaded in by typing **HELLO** and their procedures saved when they typed in **GOODBYE**. It's a fairly sophisticated system, so all the enabling software could be buried, unlike the Commodore system. That is why I prefer Apple LOGO for young children, even though the Commodore system gives children some facilities which aren't available through the Apple.

At one point last year I was given an Atari to add to the Apple, so by the end of the year we had two systems available. By then the children had abandoned the floor Turtle in favour of the screen.

The Commodore allows you to use either at the same time, but with the Apple you have to choose the floor or the screen.

In retrospect I would have appreciated being able to use the floor Turtle for longer with some of the children. Some were being held back because the floor Turtle is slow, but others need it still. The Commodore screen mirrors what the floor Turtle is doing and eventually some children notice that the picture on the screen is a copy of what they are drawing on the floor, but most remain oblivious since what they are really concerned with is what the floor Turtle is drawing.'

# LOGO encourages independent learning

'There are a lot of fundamental advantages to working with LOGO, not just for the children, but for me as a teacher. One is that inevitably, because the systems run in the classroom alongside everything else that is going on, I can give very little time to it, so the children have to develop some kind of independence. They have to learn how to handle something on their own and make it work.

They told a visitor at the end of last year that they liked LOGO because they were the teacher. It's an issue of control, which is a huge area. How much control do children have in a normal classroom? Very little. LOGO, at least the way I've been using it, gives them a considerable amount of control. That is one of its most fundamental virtues.

The children have to be initiators — nothing happens to the computer unless they do something, unlike most other sorts of software, especially drill and practice stuff. Even database and adventure games only give them partial control, but with LOGO it's all up to them. Yet they have a language with a lot of power and a definite, consistent structure, much more consistent than a teacher, who can say the same thing in a hundred different ways.

They can build up their knowledge the way they want to go, rather than being constantly pulled back by the way the teacher is seeing things. The fundamental thing it taught me was that I could let go of children.

We tend to say things like, 'Oh they are not quite the way I want them to be yet', of a class. Before I met LOGO I was asked whether I would be able to let go of the children. I was a bit worried that I might not be able to do it, but in fact I can and it has taught me a lot about the potential of children that I might not have learned without it.

Other pluses are language skills and cooperative skills. The number in the group (two at present), the male/female mixture, and the matching up of abilities, are all interesting issues which have changed throughout the year as the children have changed. As they have become more comfortable and fluent with LOGO they have become more flexible about who they work with at a particular time, or for a particular project.

The groups change quite frequently, usually by agreement. The children tend to ask if they want to work with a different partner. They seem to be able to sense intuitively when they need a change.

I always make sure, by the way, that if a pair who have been working together move off to other partners, each of them takes a copy of the procedures they have worked on jointly, so that they can use them in the new partnership. That is something they are very keen on. They don't want to lose work that they have put effort into.

If they are particularly interested in something that is happening, they may sit in on it for a while. That is possible because an infant classroom tends to be very flexible, so ten minutes watching other people work is perfectly possible. In a more formal set-up LOGO tends to get time-tabled as a subject and that sort of sharing is less likely to take place.'

## Encouraging children to talk and think

'The fact that the children are using a powerful and sophisticated tool which is theirs, and are doing this with other children, develops their social skills. The mathematical language which comes out of using the floor Turtle is fascinating to listen to. In the talk about estimating they reveal a lot of skill verbally that you might not be aware they had without LOGO to highlight it.

I remember during the first couple of weeks watching some children playing and exploring with the floor Turtle. I felt as though I had a main line into the way they were thinking for the first time. It was very exciting. You could almost see the children's thoughts, like a fourth dimension or a sixth sense, or something.

It was fascinating if you happened to be around just at the point where the child was about to solve a problem they had set themselves. It was invaluable for them to be able to find out that it's the process of figuring out the solution that's important.

I would watch the children aim for a certain thing, find that it had gone wrong and either capitalise on the error to turn the drawing into something else, or go back and debug it so that they could complete their original goal. What they were learning there were problem-solving skills, how to handle the unknown, which is fundamental to the whole process of education. It's a skill that is going to stand them in good stead whatever they are going to be learning about.'

## Editing to improve their work

'By the end of the year it had spilled over into their creative writing. About a third of the class had begun to edit their work spontaneously, which is a big step. They would come and say, 'Look, I've written a story but I've edited it in a different colour because I want to make it better'.

I had introduced the idea to one or two of them in a general way. But because they were used to the idea from working with the LOGO editor when they wanted to change their procedures and improve them, they found it an easy idea to accept and responded very readily and enthusiastically after that little push from me.

I had done some language work the previous year with some very fluent and creative seven year olds. We were looking at what they had written and discussing how to edit it to make the story flow more smoothly. That group had refused to accept any such suggestion. They were willing to listen to the idea in theory, but they just would not do it in practice. They did not want their stories changed.

But this year's group, of about the same age, and at roughly the same time of the year, were actually writing something, then looking at it critically and constructively and saying, 'I can make this better'.

I don't have scientific proof, but they do seem to be able to accept this more readily and positively than others I've taught.

The only disadvantages and frustrations I have found have been when the machines go wrong. Any other organisational hiccups, sorting out of groups, for instance, were of the sort that might happen whenever you introduce something new. Since I run an integrated day it fitted in as just another activity.

The social side is important and I wouldn't want them to work alone at the screen. They'd be more likely then to get buried in their own project and only communicate when they wanted help or information.

If I were advising other teachers I would say that the first thing to do is to make friends with LOGO yourself. Never mind the children, get to know it at your own level. That's probably true for any new activity, but particularly for LOGO. But you don't become familiar with a new reading scheme at your own level in quite the way you play with LOGO.'

## Don't panic — the children will help you

'One of the basic rules I tell my colleagues in Haringey is, 'Don't panic'. I'm joking slightly, but I honestly can't think of anything which sums it up better. The children will show you what to do if you get stuck. They often end up knowing more than you do.

Last year's class developed some pretty sophisticated non-graphic procedures. They made up a conversation procedure for me to use which asked me questions and, depending on the answer, then asked more questions. They wrote quizzes and ended up well away from graphics. They certainly got well ahead of me.

The need for list processing, which they used, had become clear when we began writing poems for Mothering Sunday and they were able to use LOGO to compose the poems; print them out and make copies to stick in their cards. (Note: this is also possible with a word-processing program like Wordwise.) They also use it to write letters to people. When Richard Noss, the Chiltern adviser, became a father, they sent him a letter. It's an easy thing to use. You use the square brackets and inside the brackets you put a list of things you want to say, which can be words as well as figures.

I know that a lot of primary teachers may be frightened off by the idea of mathematics, and the name *Turtle geometry* may put them off even more, but they don't need to be worried. LOGO helps the children to handle basic mathematical ideas like numbers and arithmetic, for example, that you are familiar with, but that you wouldn't be able to give them at a pencil and paper level.'

## Should I intervene?

'For instance, a little girl drew a chair with the floor Turtle. She had never used a procedure before and she took it to show to another teacher. The teacher said, 'I wonder if you could draw three chairs for the three bears for me. I'd love to have it for my wall'.

When she came back and told me, I realised that this was an opportunity to introduce the idea of inputs and variables. I agonised for a day over whether to do it or not, because you don't talk about variables to young children, then I decided to go ahead. It would have been criminal to have missed the opportunity.

I didn't think that most of the children would really grasp it so I left it open ended. I explained that you could make a procedure and then vary it to produce three pictures which were all the same, except that each was a different size. I then said that anyone who wanted to find out how to do it could come along and we'd do it together around the computer and we did. A lot of children took off from that, using variables in their procedures and by the end of the year they were putting two variables inside one procedure.

That experience taught me that you don't just leave LOGO to happen in a classroom. It's not a question of whether to intervene or not, it's a matter of how and when that is important. On the whole I veer towards less rather than more intervention, but the children will come along and ask you if they need help. They make LOGO into their own thing so they feel quite confident about coming and asking for help, much more so than with most classroom activities.

Most of what goes on in a classroom is teacher-instigated, even art work. LOGO isn't. The child is the instigator.'

# 5 USING DART WITH INFANTS

DART is a subset of LOGO, written in BASIC. It can be used to operate a floor Turtle and provides some of the graphics facilities of a full LOGO. It does not offer various other features such as list processing, Sprites, or music. Advanced work with full LOGO will be described later.

At Marlborough Primary and Middle School, in Harrow, North London, the infant classes share a BBC microcomputer using DART and a floor Turtle.

I spent a morning with a class of six to seven year olds. The children were working in groups at the usual mixture of infant activities — painting, sand and water play, mathematics work cards and so on. Mrs Davies, the class teacher, was supervising word matching and sentence building with a group on the carpet in the reading corner. Next to this area was the computer and floor Turtle.

Four of the red function keys on the top row of the computer had been labelled with arrows drawn on small stickers pointing in the relevant direction. It became clear that this had been done to enable the children to put in commands without having to type out entire words. A matching set of cards was available for the children to use, as I saw demonstrated later. The Turtle had eyes glued to its front and its pen was retracted.

## Finding the Fantastic Mr Fox

On the floor, was a large sheet of white card on which a looping path had been drawn out. A series of circles was drawn at various stages along the path and labelled Rabbit's burrow, Mole's, Badger's and Fox's homes. At the end of the road was the house of Fantastic Mr Fox.

There were four in the computer group. One, a girl, was writing down the commands on a piece of paper. One boy typed in the instructions on the keyboard, which were being given to him by the first girl, while another boy held the Turtle's cable to stop it getting wound too tight or tangled up as the buggy rotated. The fourth child, a girl, just watched.

The conversation went roughly like this:

'Why not move 300 and see what happens?' said one boy.

'400', said the girl, clutching her jumper to her chest.

The Turtle began to move from its starting point along the drawn track.

'It's going to go off course', said a boy, which it duly did, running right off the top of the sheet of paper.

'Back', said a boy, typing in **BACK 100**.

He explained to me what was supposed to happen. 'We are supposed to go from home to the end without going over the red lines. To make it go you press this key' (indicating the key labelled with an arrow for forward) 'then you choose a number and press **RETURN**. If you want to go right you press an arrow then **RETURN**.'

The group decided that Mr Fox, the Turtle, had gone too far so they pressed the key for **BACKWARD** and then **90**.

'We can go into the rabbit burrow and then turn.'

'When we have had three goes we change jobs', they explained and without any argument the note-maker, cable-holder, programmer and watcher, swapped round.

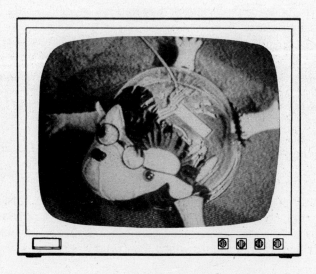

*The Jessop floor Turtle converted to Fantastic Mr Fox.*

The girl now in charge of programming couldn't figure out which direction she wanted to order the Turtle to turn. She chose an arrow, put it in front of the floor Turtle, read the word *right* written on the card beneath the arrow then pressed the key labelled with the arrow to show **RIGHT** followed by a number.

'**FORWARD 100**', she said, typing in the command. The Turtle moved off.

'A bit more', said someone.

'All right, **FORWARD 20**.'

The watcher, a lively boy, was by now squirming on the floor, paying close attention to what was happening, but unable to stand still.

The girl at the keyboard picked up the *left* direction card, put it beside the Turtle, decided it wasn't the direction she wanted, so chose the one saying *right*.

'Forward 300?'

'No.'

After discussion, they decided that 400 might be correct, but she insisted on putting in 300 because last time they had put in 400 and the Turtle had run off the board.

300 turned out to be absolutely correct. The Turtle had now reached a corner on the road.

She decided to type in **LEFT 90**. I asked her how she knew that was the correct amount.

'We learnt the first time we used the Turtle that 90 is the correct amount to turn.'

In fact later they managed to put in a **LEFT 40** to enable the Turtle to navigate a cunning little kink in the track which was not a right-angle turn. Clearly they have some sense of the connection between the size of the number and the degree of turn which the Turtle will make.

Throughout the session the children worked harmoniously, thinking before they moved, checking the direction before they put in the instructions, using the **DELETE** button when they put in the wrong instruction by mistake.

The fact that they were infants showed up in their difficulty in keeping the paper recording straight. The very active boy had written down the instructions in a random fashion all over the paper, in typical infant fashion, and I had to rescue him by rewriting them in sequence.

They seemed oblivious of the fact that the screen Turtle was drawing out a path identical with the one that the pen-less Turtle was making.

Occasionally, there was a certain amount of mischievous cheating, like turning the Turtle around when the programmer's back was turned, or heaving it bodily to the correct point on the track. But an impressive amount of learning was taking place in a remarkably orderly and amiable fashion, without any supervision.

Their teacher remained within earshot, but intervened only to adjudicate turns at the end, when the Turtle had nearly reached Mr Fox's home. She allowed everybody one final go and they were able to sort that out by taking the Turtle forward in short steps, such as 50 or 20, so that everybody could have a share in the arrival.

## Starting to use DART

Kath Davies explained how she had started the class off:

'I have used DART for two years, but with this class it's only been going for a year. We have the Turtle one day a week and they use it in groups of four.

Each group has it for about 20 minutes. I don't keep too strictly to the time. If they haven't got to the end of the track by then I don't stop them.

At first they started off by experimenting with the floor Turtle to find out about the commands and the idea of turning and by how much they should turn. Initially, they would order it to move by units of one or two, but gradually they came to see that that was too short to be effective.

Then I would set them a challenge. I would put a circle round the Turtle marked *home*, then put up some bricks as an obstacle or a roundabout in the middle of the paper and say, 'Can you get him round the roundabout and back to home again?'

When they got proficient at moving it round without bashing it into obstacles, we would draw a track onto the paper with different turns in it and they would have to get it from home to a certain destination (such as a shop or animal) which they could choose.

Usually the plan is connected to our topic or a story we are reading at the time. At the moment we are doing *Underground* as our topic, so the Turtle is Mr Fox, going underground, round the rabbit's burrow and badger's sett and so on.'

## The classroom benefits of using LOGO

'I find LOGO a very useful part of my classroom activity. It has a lot of unique things about it. In particular, I like the effect it has on working in groups. Getting six and seven year olds to work cooperatively in a group is something that rarely happens. Even if they are playing a game together, which is a very structured thing to do, or if you are trying to get them to work cooperatively in maths or have a discussion, for example, at this age it usually disintegrates if you're not actually there with them.

With this Turtle work you actually hear them arguing, 'I don't think it's that, I think it's this' and working in a way where they have three turns each and then rotate. It takes a while to get to that point of cooperation, but it does happen after a bit and this is quite a young age for that to take place.

I like the logic involved and the planning; being able to predict what is going to happen. There are not a lot of other activities that involve all those things.

In maths, estimating distance and turn are valuable. They see, for example, that 200 may get the Turtle halfway to the point they are aiming for, so they have to start thinking how to get him the rest of the way. Can we do it in one go or not? They have grasped the actual idea of angles as a degree of turn, even though we don't call them angles at this stage.

Every few weeks I have a class session. At the moment we are trying to work out the fewest possible moves to get from home to the destination. It's valuable for some of them to have had to think beforehand and to have a challenge set for them, like trying to get as close to the minimum number as possible. Some of them find driving the Turtle very easy after a while and they need something to stretch them.

I think this type of work is preferable to using the computer for number games which are fun, but no different from things you could do at a table.

At the next stage they will start putting the pen in the Turtle and leaving a track. That becomes a bit more abstract so they do that in the next call.

From tracks they move on to drawing pictures and shapes and then they can go on to the screen.'

## Staff training and help

'As far as training and backup go, all the first school teachers here had a little meeting with Deborah, who was the computer person on the staff. We discussed how we would start off with LOGO in our classrooms and really, we all learned as we went along.

All we knew at the beginning was how we were going to get our children started, taking it very much from the infant teacher's standpoint. We talked about how we were going to get them to use the keyboard. We were going to need some sort of symbolism because it would take them too long to type in **FORWARD** all the time. We decided which symbols to use for **FORWARD, BACKWARD** and so on and decided to have the red function keys at the top adapted so that they could *write* **FORWARD**, for example, simply by pressing one key.

After this we had to talk about how we would get them to understand things like turning, and developed strategies for introducing it in movement lessons first.

There were lots of teething troubles at first. When you typed in a command, sometimes nothing would happen, but we found out how to cope. Sometimes the children would press the key too hard, for instance, but they adjusted to that. There are lots of other symbols for things like **BUILD**, which I am not sure how to use, but as I'm with the young ones, we haven't needed to use them.'

## Management problems

'If we had a machine just to ourselves they would get on faster and have longer turns each time, but at the moment I'm happy to just plan for the one day. Sometimes it is disruptive to have a group called away for their turn just when I'm in the middle of explaining something to them. That sort of thing could be avoided if I had a machine all the time because I wouldn't need to use it so solidly.

We did find that it was more hassle than it was worth, introducing LOGO to the reception and second year children: they were too young to work unsupervised in groups and the teacher was having to stand with them by the computer all day.

If we had separate classes for the fives and sixes you could probably start off the second years. It's the rising fives that are the problem. The little ones are all right together in a big group with you, as a class lesson, but we found that they couldn't cope on their own so we leave it till they are six-plus or seven at the moment. I think that what we are probably going to do now is use the summer term to give the children coming up some experience.

I do think that it is very important that children have a lot of experience with the floor Turtle before they move on to the screen. If they have actually seen a solid object moving right at the beginning, they can relate that to their own bodies. It's no different from any other subject with infants. You start with the concrete.'

## Another teacher's view

I talked to Mrs Evelyn Hanney who also teaches six to seven year olds and used the Turtle with DART.

'I am very impressed by it. One of the most beneficial things about it is the way the children have to learn to work together without quarrelling, using discussion and logic.

I try to make my groups mixed ability. The children benefit from the mixture. Oddly enough the able ones don't always dominate because they are not necessarily the most proficient on the computer. Often the ones who are not particularly good at recording work are very good at working out where they want to go physically, in space. They can be better at orientating their own bodies in the right direction, for example, so they can steer the Turtle accurately. Often it's also the less able ones who seem to have a better grasp of distance and who are the more observant. It may be because the brighter children are always in a hurry to show that they can do something, while the slower child is more meticulou

It hasn't disrupted my class routine at all. We have a rule that if someone interferes with the group working at the computer then they lose their turn.

I would welcome the chance to have a Turtle full time in my classroom. It would allow the children to have longer turns and the capable ones would be able to develop more quickly.'

At first the staff had the computer in the staffroom. For about three weeks they played with it at break or lunchtimes.

Another teacher told me, 'I introduce it initially to the class as a whole, then split them up into groups. Every few weeks I bring them back together to discuss what they have learned and to reinforce ideas. After a few weeks' experience they have noticed, for example, that FORWARD 10 is hardly going to move the Turtle any distance at all. So we discuss what that means.

I can't say that they are dealing with large numbers any more quickly since using the Turtle. Normally infants don't deal in numbers up to a hundred and though they will talk about 100, all they really mean is that it is a big gap, whereas ten is a small gap. Their grasp of the idea is still pretty vague. The number is really just a symbol.

An HMI came in to visit the class while they were working with the computer one day and he said that he had never seen a group of young children working together so well.

I was very frightened of the computer when it first came in. I was sure that I'd never be able to use it. I'm near retiring age and at first I was terrified and thought, 'I'll never get the hang of this'. I'm not at all science-minded, but my confidence was built up gradually. When I saw how much the children enjoyed it, I suppose I just learned with them.'

*An experienced teacher explores LOGO with her pupils.*

# Infants to juniors:
# the middle range

*See page 195 for the program to produce these birds.*

# 6 FROM BIG TRAK TO THE FLOOR TURTLE

A number of infant classes at Green Close School continue with and develop the work using Big Trak which starts in the nursery. The two parallel first and second year infant classes use Big Trak on its own.

Christine Caswell uses Big Trak with her six to seven year olds and then they move on to the floor Turtle. On the day I visited two groups of children were working with Big Traks. The second group had set out a number problem using cardboard numbers.

**3 + 2 = ?**

They were sending Big Trak along a path made up of cut-out Trak shapes, numbered from zero to five. The plan was to program it to move number three, pause, then move on two more lengths. The total would be read off when it stopped.

A road with a level crossing flanked by two model people had been drawn on card and put on the carpet. One group was trying to program the tank with a set of instructions which would make it go along the road, pause at the zebra crossing, then move on.

## A teacher's introduction to Big Trak

A group of three was using the floor Turtle to draw out a shape on paper. Christine explained the background:

'I teach a class of top infants, six and seven year olds. There are 21 in the class, 13 boys and eight girls.

I became involved with the Walsall LOGO Project quite early on because Linda Spear, an experienced infant teacher who was joint coordinator, came to Green Close and started by showing the Big Trak to the staff one day after school.

It was a very hot July afternoon near the end of term and we were all saying, 'Oh, what's all this?' but as soon as I saw it I thought, 'That's wonderful'. It presents something I can really use in the classroom.

Linda started working in the school in September and actually came to my classroom to work with my class in groups. She took two groups of three, six altogether at a time, and I had another half-a-dozen.

We'd change over while she was there, so we each had the use of the carpeted area in the room. She took the less able ones and I took the quicker ones.

*A group of teachers exploring the educational benefits of Big Trak.*

It wasn't the case that I could follow what she was doing. We worked independently, though she was there to support me and give me ideas, but really, I suppose I took off on my own with Big Trak because from the beginning I could see that it was a valuable tool in itself, apart from its value in leading to LOGO, because of the fun the children had using it without realising the thinking that was involved.

I had a booklet that Linda had written explaining the function keys, but I just took Big Trak home and played with it a couple of times in order to keep ahead of the children. Those sessions helped me to some extent as I also learned with the children.

This September I had children who had had a little Big Trak experience in the middle infants which I had been able to give them in my non-class-based time. They all arrived knowing about **FORWARD** and **BACKWARD** and understood the idea of making a simple program.

That really gave me a head start for getting into LOGO. Last year it had taken me till the summer term to get children using the floor Turtle. This year they were ready by the end of the first half-term.'

## Using Big Trak as preparation for the floor Turtle

'I also realised that some children didn't need as much Big Trak as preparation for LOGO as others. In that respect it's like other work, reading activities, for example: some come in ready to read, others need preparatory activities.

So to begin with I concentrated on measuring distances so they got the idea of the Big Trak's length. I very soon got on to the idea of rotation, because you need to do that to use LOGO.

Even now I have some that aren't ready for that yet. They can't work out the left/right turns correctly without pointing and they don't seem to remember from one time to the next, so I don't think they are ready for the floor Turtle.

Last year I let the children play with Big Trak quite a lot. It was more of an activity available if they had finished their work, to play with and see what they could do. This year I direct the children far more in what they do. I haven't allowed it as free play: it's been part of a specific learning situation. They look on it as part of their work with problems I set.

I put them in threes according to general ability and try to give them a task which means they are going to have to work together. It might not be that difficult; they may only have to move the Big Trak along a path a certain number of lengths, but they have to cooperate.

At first I found that the person whose turn it was to program the Big Trak was doing everything and though they were supposed to be working in a group the others weren't involved. Now I use a system which I think works much better and makes sure that they have to communicate with each other.

For example, when they are using the road, one child gives the order, one types in the program and the third has to design the course for Big Trak to move along. I have an egg-timer and when the sand runs through they have to switch roles. It carries on independently of me and they enjoy that. The person with the most passive job also watches the egg-timer.

I do the same with the floor Turtle trios. The lead holder is also the time-keeper, number two looks at the Turtle, decides what to do and instructs the third person, who is on the keyboard.

I am the one who decides when a child is ready to move on to the Turtle. I don't know if that is necessarily right. It's just the way I am. Some teachers might think that is wrong. It just depends how you operate. I do think you need to make sure that they are clear about things like Big Trak length and rotation before they move on to the floor Turtle.'

## Children starting to use the floor Turtle

'As far as introducing the children to the floor Turtle is concerned we do it in threes. Sometimes the class is working as a whole, but if they are doing something like language work in groups, for example, then that would be a time that I would be able to work with a group, say on Big Trak.

It's something which is spread over weeks and the time I can give it varies a lot. I couldn't say there would be any set times which I could count on being able to spend on it, but I aim to give every child in the class some time with Big Trak or the floor Turtle during a week. It doesn't always happen, but that is the aim. On my timetable, I've actually got written down Monday — groups one and two; Tuesday — groups three and four, and so on. I've slotted it in where it ought to be because I think the discipline of doing it like that makes it more likely that I'll do it rather than not even deciding where I'm going to start.

I don't stick to it rigidly. I have the floor Turtle all day Tuesday and for an hour Julian Pixton, the Walsall coordinator, comes in and I work with him. That's exciting because he brings in another floor Turtle so there is great one-upmanship between the two groups. If mine see that his are doing circles they want to know how that works. It's really smashing because his expertise has really egged us on a bit.

I have also used the Turtle graphics booklet which Walsall has produced. I helped write the one about Big Trak. They offer you lots of ideas for starting points which is useful.'

## The benefits of using LOGO

'I think the biggest advantage my children get from using LOGO, as far as their learning is concerned, is something which is part of my philosophy of teaching right across the board. It isn't just something which comes from LOGO, but LOGO has certainly helped.

What LOGO enables the children to do is to learn how to cooperate with each other. They are having to negotiate, they are having to plan, and to communicate wth each other. That's not something they can learn working in isolation from each other on things like comprehension cards.

I do try to arrange that sort of experience with other activities, but I do find that this is particularly — I wouldn't say easy — but it lends itself particularly well to cooperative learning. In other situations you may think you've got the children working together in groups and interacting with each other, but in actual fact they can still be working in isolation, in what looks like a group.

I can't honestly tell at the moment what effect LOGO is having on their mathematics. I think it's making the brighter children think more clearly. I suppose it is with the others too. But I couldn't be sure. I think it has had some effect on their language development because of the fact that they communicate better, which carries over into their written work.

At the moment they are a bit restricted in the sort of things they try to draw with the floor Turtle. Because they are just learning to cope with terms like *repeat* and *procedure*, they tend mainly to stick to houses and rectangular-shaped things, which is a bit limiting. They are still having to concentrate on learning to work together as a team. That is probably the most important thing for them to get right. By the summer term I think they will get on faster with building interesting procedures.

Working on LOGO, the children are forced to interact and to listen to each other's opinions. It has also made it easier to spot those who are still a little bit immature. I know they are only six and seven, but some can work together and others just can't. They want it to be their way because they are still so young. They just don't want to change their ideas once they have made up their minds.

Having to change jobs every few minutes makes each one learn to fall in with the others. That, to me, is really the most important side of it.'

# 7 FROM 'FROGGO' TO THE SCREEN

Linda Spear, an experienced primary teacher, was seconded to the Walsall LOGO Project for 18 months then returned to class teaching.

I paid two visits to her class of seven to eight year olds — a first year junior class — at Hillary Junior School in Walsall.

Most of the children in this inner city school are Asian and top-knots and tunics combine with strong Birmingham accents. The children work at tables in small groups, doing a variety of different tasks — English, mathematics, reading, painting.

On the walls are drawings, including some of a Big Trak, collage work, and some paintings 'in the style of Paul Gauguin'.

On arrival I was given a cup of tea and a selection of the cakes which another class had made to sell in aid of Ethiopia. After finding out who I was and why I had come everyone went back to work. Linda was almost invisible, sitting on the carpet with a group of readers while the others got on with their various activities.

## Big Trak is converted to Froggo

The class has a Big Trak which has been turned into a Froggo, with a green shell and big eyes. Linda explained that this less warlike and aggressive model suited the ethos of her class better than had the original tank.

Three girls were sending Froggo round an obstacle course of bricks. They seemed to be working well together, with a great deal of harmonious conversation and consultation as they put Froggo through his paces.

At the BBC computer another group, consisting of a girl and two boys, was using the floor Turtle to draw out a house and garage.

One group of boys used their turn to draw things they were individually interested in. Vishnu was making a V, which he decided to turn into Vi. He instructed the Turtle to **FORWARD 80 RIGHT 90 RIGHT 78 LEFT 34** and so on.

Then the group decided to turn something that had started out as an S into a hexagon.

Both groups of children were able to explain what they were doing calmly and independently.

On my second visit, three months later, a group of girls were making some pictures for a competition on good health. They were discussing what the first prize was likely to be. One of them remarked that it was unlikely to be a box of chocolates for the prize since that's not good for your health — but this idea did not seem to put them off trying!

Others were measuring the circumferences of heads in an attempt to work out whether there is much difference between the size of a child's head and that of an adult. I was duly measured.

Three groups of children were involved with computer work. One group was working with Froggo, a group of three were using the BBC with a floor Turtle and two girls were busy at an Atari.

## Froggo on his pond

The three girls with Froggo were kneeling on the corner carpet. Stretched out in front of them was an old roller blackboard on which a pond had been painted, complete with lily pads, and a clump of frog spawn. A large forked branch sat in one corner of the pond.

What were they up to, I asked.

'We are going to make a map and all the children in our class are going to have to try to make Froggo go all the way around using the instructions on the map.'

Apparently, they had worked out a set of moves which Froggo would need to make in order to move in stages from the starting point, a lily pond leaf, under the branch, stopping on another lily leaf and ending up on its *babbies*, the frog spawn. As they had worked out the course, one girl had noted down the moves. The rest of the class would be given a map of the course they should follow, but the actual program would be kept a secret.

The starting point for this activity had been a visit to the school by *the animal man* who brings in unusual creatures for the children to look at and hold. This term's specimens had included a bull frog, which gave them the idea for the pond project.

The girls had made up a story to go with their game which they read to me.

'Once there lived a frog and he said to himself I think I'll go on a journey, so off he went. I'll go and see my babbies first, so he did. Then he went on his journey. He started on the mud then he went under the twisted branch then he went to lily pond leaves, then on a safe place, then under a obstacle then on to a leaf, then on to his babbies, then on another leaf then he went back home.'

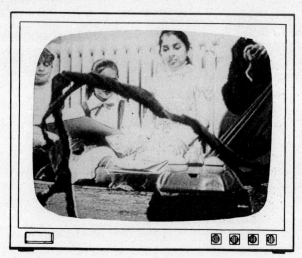

*Froggo (a converted Big Trak) moving round his pond*

## Drawing a rocket with the screen Turtle

I went up to the group working on the screen. This was only their second attempt to work without the floor Turtle. One was a girl, Jatinda; the two boys were Ravinder and Adrian. The discussion went roughly like this:

Me: 'What are you doing?'

Jatinda: 'Please Miss what's your name?'

Me: 'I'm Mrs Anderson — or Beverly if you like.'

Adrian: 'We are playing with the computer and making a rocket.'

They had drawn a plan on a bit of paper. While I was looking at it someone else came up to measure my head. The various parts of the rocket had been labelled *body*, *nose*, *wings* and *fire*. Clearly they had decided to break the picture down into sections and draw it a bit at a time.

Adrian was giving the orders, Ravinder was typing them in and Jatinda, whose job was to write down the sequence of instructions on paper, also acted as commentator. They were working in direct drive, experimenting with commands, but not trying to save their procedures. The triangular-shaped nose of the rocket was to be the first step.

Adrian: 'Let's do forward five.'

Ravinder: 'Yeah. Forward! Forward five.'

Jatinda: 'Look! you haven't done it. It's going to bend!'

Adrian: 'I told you I was going to do it right!'

Jatinda: 'Left!'

Ravinder: 'No. Down.'

Jatinda (very excited): 'Backwards, yes backwards!'

Adrian: 'Yes.'

Me (unable to resist interfering): 'You want it to go backwards now?'

Ravinder: 'Eight.'

Julian: 'Ten.'

Ravinder: 'Oh no! It's going backwards that way! We should have gone that way and go downwards.'

Adrian: 'Turn right again.'

Ravinder: 'Right.'

Julian: 'Head back now.'

Ravinder: 'Which number?'

Adrian: 'Eight again.'

Jatinda: 'Eight again! You won't . . . . it will go back straight!'

Me: 'You want it to go far over to the right, do you?'

Jatinda: 'We want it to go like that. How far do you think it should go?'

Ravinder: 'I think it must be going five.'

Me: 'You think five, so what are you going to do? Will you try right five and see how far he will turn?'

Ravinder: 'Right five.'

Jatinda: 'YEEES! It's done it.'

Julian: 'YEAHHH!'

Ravinder: 'Right again.'

Jatinda and Adrian: 'Right!'

Ravinder: 'Right five again. Right five.' (Types it in.)

Jatinda and Adrian: 'Yes. Yes!'

Ravinder (in a tone of quiet pleasure): 'I did it right.'

Julian: 'Make it go forward.'

Ravinder: 'Forward.'

Jatinda: 'Yes, forward.'

Julian: 'Forward five?'

Ravinder: 'Five.' (Types it in.)

Jatinda: 'Yes. Space!' (To remind him that there has to be a gap between forward and the number.)

Ravinder: 'I did space.'

Julian: 'Return!'

Ravinder: 'Forward five.'

Jatinda: 'EEEEEAAAGGH!'

Julian: 'It's like an ice.'

After some confusion about the correct bit of paper to record on, who it belonged to, then borrowing someone else's, they got back to trying to make the cone.

Ravinder: 'Forward three again.'

Jatinda: 'Did you press return?'

Ravinder laughs and does so.

Ravinder: 'Right?'

Julian: 'Right three.'

Ravinder repeats as he types: 'Right three.'

Jatinda: 'Space!'

Julian: 'Mistake. Hey! Pen down!'

Jatinda: 'HAUUUGH! My God! We have to get all of that off and do it again.'

After several minutes of activity:

Jatinda: 'AUU! Look at that!'

(The screen reports to them `RT DOESN'T LIKE 9 RT AS INPUT`.)

Me: 'So what are you going to do now?'

Julian: 'We have to do CS, CS.' (For clear screen.)

All agree on the need to press the keys for CS.

'Return!' they chorus.

By now it is Jatinda's turn to man the keyboard. They carry on the discussion for several more minutes.

Two of the children are seven and the third is eight today. They are obviously still settling down as a working team and have only a very limited grasp as yet of how to make a shape in direct drive on the screen. But they clearly understand what instructions must be put in and how to use such items as **CS**, **RETURN** and **ERASE**. There is some frustration, a fair amount of confusion, but no distress. Trying to make the rocket's cone appears to be an exciting challenge although they are finding it difficult to produce the shape they want.

## Their teacher joins in

After a while Linda leaves her group of readers and goes over to talk with them about the rocket and to give them a hand. She asks them what they want to do and tries to get them to suggest what might be the next step rather than telling them the answer.

Linda: 'Now what you going to tell it to do?'

All three: 'Right.'

Linda: 'And what will that make it do? Will it make it draw a line?'

Chorus: 'Yeah!'

Linda: 'That'll make it draw a line if I turn it right?'

Chorus: 'Yeah!'

Linda: 'Go on then. Right what?'

'70.'

'Has that drawn a line? What do you want it to do now?'

'Forward 70?'

'Jatinda says forward 70. Is that right Jatinda?'

'Yes!'

'Is that going to draw the nose?'

'Right.'

'Why do you say right?'

'But if you said forward where will it go?'

'He says if you go forward it will go to the top of the screen.'

'Is that right Jatinda?'

'Yes.'

'So what's he got to do with it first Adrian?'

'He's got to turn it right.'

'Fine. Swap over now.'

Two eight year old boys are trying to make a car. They have made a plan on paper then tried it out in direct drive on the Atari computer.

Linda explains:

'That group of boys started off with an instant program. They had worked extensively with the floor Turtle and they wanted to transfer to screen Turtle but found the numbers very difficult to operate, so I introduced an instant program which is a one-key press for forward right and left. They used that to draw up a list of instructions.

They eventually noticed that whenever they pressed **FORWARD**, the distance the Turtle moved stayed the same, in other words that the one-key press was a set of constants. Now that they have understood that development I've said that they can redraw the car, take it out of this one-key press procedure and redraw it putting in their own numbers, so they can check it themselves.'

## Creating a garden using Sprites

Harjit and her friend Shelley used the Atari to make a procedure called GARDEN.

Harjit: 'We made a garden on the Atari, with flowers and a girl walking along picking the flowers.'

Shelley: 'Mrs Spear's got to check it out because something's gone wrong with the people.'

Harjit: 'But you can still see the garden. Clear screen. Put in 'to garden'. Then space. No.'

The screen says **I DON'T KNOW HOW TO GARDEN**. They try **3GARDEN** which works. The Turtle draws out a rectangle with flowers all the way round.

The flowers were made through a subprocedure.

Shelley: 'They were sort of circles but we couldn't make the proper shape see, so we had to do . . .'

Harjit: 'When we made that shape we thought it was quite good so we said we would do it and these are all the inputs to it we got.'

Shelley: 'Now we're making people.'

Me: 'How far have you got?'

Shelley: 'Well, Mrs Spear can't load it in properly. It won't load in.'

Linda: 'It does it. It just keeps going off every now and then. It's my fault because when I saved it, I saved it inside a procedure instead of leaving it as a variable. They didn't understand, but because they want to do these moving pictures I obviously have got to get to the stage where I can explain it to them.'

In order to correct the bugs in the people she typed in **ED SHAPE** for edit shape. The mistake turned out to be a simple one.

Linda: 'We've done it!'

Harjit: 'She forgot to put pen up — that was all.'

The girls used the Sprite facility for the people in their garden. A Sprite is an object which can appear on the screen and can be coloured or plain. It takes the form of a grid 16 by 16 which can be used to make different shapes. Each square can be coloured in by pressing a key, or can be left blank. Once the shape has been drawn out and given a number the Sprite then acts like a Turtle. It can be ordered to move at a particular speed or in a particular direction so that it can be used for animations.

*The Sprite above is carrying the shape of a dog. Whatever the shape, once in the editor, it can be changed and movement created.*

The girls were drawing the outline of a woman in a short skirt, discussing it as they went along.

By the end of the period the nose cone for the rocket had been made. They were going on to make a rectangle for the body.

I asked the girls whether they minded making mistakes. They said, 'No, it doesn't matter if we make a mistake because we can always do it again'.

I asked the rocket group whether mistakes were important. 'No', they said. 'We put in delete, and if we want to clear it, we put CS.'

Me: 'Is it easier than clearing up a mistake on paper?'

'Oh yes. It's easy peazy lemon squeezy.'

## Talking to the class teacher

After the children had gone home I talked to Linda Spear about what I had seen.

Her class had had a Turtle for three-and-a-half weeks when I saw them in November, and had had a Big Trak since September. Jatinda had made a drawing of a house on her first go with the floor Turtle.

Linda suggested that for the teacher who wanted to make a start it might be useful to have a good Turtle graphics package and sample it before deciding on a full LOGO system.

As far as spillover work was concerned, in language the children showed an increased ability to review and edit their written work. Linda keeps a diary of the children's work and relationships using a record sheet.

She had noticed that groups working with the Froggo seemed to find it easier to tolerate their mistakes and adapt to them than they did when working with the Turtle. On the other hand, the slowness and inaccuracy of the Big Trak became frustrating to many after a while.

## Introducing children to LOGO work

*Had she been able to detect any particular sequence of development? Could she suggest an order for proceeding?*

'I would recommend that you start in the nursery and very small infants with the Big Trak — really just to play and to explore. You could probably adapt the keyboard and have matching activities where you cover over the numbers and have colour matching or picture matching and build resources around that. The value of using small robots at first, unconnected to a computer is that, like the children, they run in free space.

It has a dual purpose at the next stage. You can begin to lead into things like number work. Big Trak does lend itself to that more readily in the early stages, but you have to take it away and play with it as well — as a free activity — like LEGO®.

When you get to the middle or top infants you can encourage a lot more planning around Big Trak, such as in the Froggo game which started when the animal man made his visit. The story is only in its bare bones at the moment, but the children are planning to make a zigzag book with it. In order to send Froggo round the course the children have had to be involved with number all the time, but number is not the major part of it. What they are doing is creating a whole little world.

Out of that comes quite naturally the idea that numbers are arbitrary units. That is an important concept for them to grasp when dealing with units of measurement.'

LEGO is a registered trademark

*When did you decide to move to the floor Turtle?*

'The children do it. They get frustrated by Froggo and say, 'It doesn't do exactly what I want it to do and I'm fed up with trying to make it', and that's the time you move on. Sometimes, while they are moving through that process and have gone on to the floor Turtle they will come back and use the Big Trak.

When they are ready to use the floor Turtle I introduce it to the whole group. I show them how to set it up and take it to bits. I encourage children to come out and have a go at doing that and repeat it perhaps four or five times over a week. At first, I don't introduce the pen, I just let them move the Turtle over the floor, knocking over skittles, etc, so they get the idea that it is a moving object without emphasising it is a drawing machine.

Then we set up groups of three to work together, usually friendship groups, though preferably with at least one boy and girl per group. They are allowed to go away in their groups and come back again after 15 minutes so we can all talk together.

We work out a timetable which they can agree on and they spend about half-a-term adhering to that so that they can get used to the routine. I keep an eye on them all the time to spot when the pen can be introduced and whether they are doing the kinds of things with the Turtle which are conducive to programming (such as planning).

The first experiences the children have is with the floor Turtle and Julian Pixton's Turtle graphics package. The function keys at the top of the keyboard have arrows on them which are designated **FORWARD**, **BACKWARD**, **RIGHT** and **LEFT**. I say that they are direction keys and suggest that we explore what happens to the Turtle when we press each one. I think it is very important at the initial stage not to burden a child who is just learning to read with too much unnecessary work. If you can help them to explore by providing clues like that, they can concentrate on the experience you are really trying to offer.

They are probably ready to move to the screen when they begin to draw very large and detailed pictures with the floor Turtle and to be frustrated by the length of time it takes to draw out the shapes on the floor. I show them some of the possibilities like changing the screen colour or pen colours which some of them pick up and use.

Again, initially they should work in direct drive without trying to build procedures. Translating physical movements into lines on a screen is quite an abstract task and they need time to adapt. After making abstract shapes they tend to build up more complex projects — pictures of lorries, buses, houses, things from the real world. They break these down into little parts and build procedures for each section and eventually go on to quite complicated programs made up of a number of procedures. Since these activities are rooted in their own experience and based on their own choice they aren't as dependent on the teacher if things don't go as planned. They can decide to modify the plan to fit in with what they have actually drawn or they can change it.'

## The value of making mistakes

'The business of bugs is the most valuable part of LOGO. So much of what happens in school is a case of getting things right or wrong and your job as teacher is to make those sorts of distinctions. Through LOGO you give a child the opportunity to replace that with trial and error. Mistakes don't matter. In fact they add to the fun because we can change it and find out why it went wrong. That sets off the sort of attitude to problem solving that we all like to think prevails in our classrooms.

The group trying to make the rocket nose today and getting into a tangle, were having one of their first experiences with the screen. At first they try to do everything at once, but realise quite quickly that they can't and have to start breaking it down. That group had started to plan the rocket and had made a whole long list of instructions. As they were putting them in they realised that they weren't going to work so they went away again and started with the nose.

You've actually got to allow children to fend for themselves, and wrestle with the problem for a while. But when they are starting on something fresh you have to be very near them and be ready to come back every five or six minutes to say, 'How are you getting on?' and other salient questions. So you have to make sure that when you organise the timetable you allow for that time.

It can be quite hard for a teacher to stand back and let the child stumble. Sometimes they get quite confused and it's only at that point that you say, 'How did you get there? Explain it to me.' Many teachers would want to step in sooner, but LOGO provides a safe environment for children.

There is a limit within which they can make errors and you can be sure that they won't go too badly wrong. The language is very friendly too and it gives error messages which allow you to trace where they have made the mistake so you have some feedback and a reference point from which to help them.'

There was a very wide spread of activities and range of apparent stages of development within the one class.

*Why were the children making GARDEN much further ahead than the rest?*

'That group has developed a keen interest in LOGO. When we got the computers in and drew up the class timetable the children decided between them how many times a week they would use them and what for.

But that changes according to the project. Children who are working on the Atari need more time now. They said to the class, 'What we are trying to do is to build this garden and we want to have these people walking along' and the class agreed that they could have more time. In return there will come a time when they won't have quite as much time as some other group and they will accept that quite happily.

That pair are brighter than average and are girls. For some reason at that age girls seem to be more creative in approach and far more flexible in learning about things like Sprites. Some of the boys have seen Sprites and have been quite excited about them, but are also a little bit scared of taking them on board and working with them.

In any case it is important to keep an eye on bright children who can be quick to work out ways of skirting problems. One needs to set them examples which force them to work all the way through a procedure otherwise they are playing but not growing mentally: Sprites provide a good way in to this.'

## The benefits of LOGO work

*What sort of things do they use LOGO for?*

'Well, they make stories like the one you have seen, weaving them around things that they probably don't see very much of, like the frog environment. The rocket, the little ones are starting to draw, is based on a space adventure in their reading book. Another group is drawing Doctor Who's Tardis.

The garden came from the fact that Shelley and her mother are keen gardeners. What she would really like to do is draw different petals on the flowers. Now that is difficult and quite ambitious and I've not said to her, 'I don't think you are going to manage it.' I'm not going to say that.

They got the idea about working with the Atari when they saw me using it to do some programming for them. It is an important part of LOGO, I think, that teachers and pupils can provide each other with materials to work with, sometimes independently and sometimes together. They knew what they wanted their picture to be like and had started it tentatively on the BBC. But when they saw the Atari LOGO they thought it was much more exciting to be able to see the little creatures which they could move around. At this stage they have the flowers being drawn out and the lady going round the garden picking them.

Next they plan to develop the story aspect so I shall have to teach them how to put the text on the screen, how to scroll it round and how to stop it. I'll probably use that as a teaching session for the whole class. It will be their learning experience, but there will be things about it that everyone else will want to be shown as well, and it can be used in a variety of situations.

What impressed me was the fact that they started from the whole story and then broke it down into sections. They are obviously thinking at a different level than before.

There are other things we want to do with computers besides LOGO. We've just converted our Tandys to word processors. We have got involved in the Domesday project with the BBCs, we have got the new Spectrum which we use for simulations, and there are two Big Traks in the special needs classes which their teachers are using to develop mathematical concepts.

I think that by the summer virtually all of my class will be working on the screen Turtle. Most of them will probably only want to use Big Trak as a free activity like LEGO. There are six groups working at the moment. Maybe two or three of them will be working on the sort of thing you saw today, with four or five procedures inside one major procedure and using Sprites. The other three will probably be doing things like making individual pictures such as the Tardis.'

*What are the advantages you see for children in working with LOGO?*

'I think the first thing is attitude towards learning, working cooperatively to find information, discussing and recording work as a group. Children find that hard to do without making a lot of mistakes normally, but the LOGO environment makes it all considerably easier.

The second is that quite a lot of the boys in my class are Muslim and their attitude towards women and work and education generally is that women don't have a place in it. Well, here the boys often ask the girls for help, so that is positive.

The other thing is that when it comes to things like redrafting they will very happily sit down and cast a critical eye over their written work. Now that's very difficult for seven and eight year olds to do.

I have never given them a planning book, but they do use their maths books for planning and some of them have devised systems where they use the back of a book to do planning in. It's not standard throughout the class, it's what some of them have chosen to do. They write out their story, come and show it to me, we talk about it, they use the dictionary, go away, redraft it and do it again in the front of the book. I have tried to remain neutral, but I think this is an idea or a skill they have picked up through working with LOGO.

All primary teachers are concerned about the fact that not enough genuine problem-solving opportunities occur, not just in mathematics but in the rest of the curriculum. LOGO provides a natural and easy way in through a tiny, tidy world that the children invent and can work in. They can develop a model for solving problems in all sorts of areas of the curriculum. Perhaps the name 'problem solving' isn't really an adequate one.'

## Class organisation

'It is the case that certain types of class organisation lend themselves particularly to LOGO. You need to provide yourself and the child with a timetable which is easy to operate. You can have total fluidity in the use of the computer.

You have to have a structure around it which ensures that it's not separate from the rest of their activities and the manner in which their other work is organised. Often they work in friendship groups for other things and it happens sometimes with the LOGO groupings too where some of the so-called more able children choose to work with Froggo because they are not as confident about free exploration as some of the less able children, who are quite happily using the screen Turtle. It can be instructive for the teacher to see what attitudes the children have already developed towards learning.

I think the most difficult thing apart from the attitude, the philosophy — and this is a personal thing which teachers have to come to grips with — is organising your classroom so that as well as carrying on with all the other activities you usually provide, you allow quite a lot of time for LOGO.

Because it is quite time intensive you have to be very fair about this. The only way you can do it is to make quite sure that the children are aware of the problem and that when you create the timetable you involve them.

I keep to quite a rigid structure and a strict time. I say, 'You have had your time' and unless it is something the others agree to letting go on they have to stop. We all have to work with timescales imposed on us.'

*How much can young children do without supervision or contact with the teacher?*

'Not much. But I think that is true for every activity. Some teachers will leave children to get on with a story for say 15 minutes and they can get all wound up in a muddle with that too.

If normally as a teacher you aren't tucked away behind a desk, but are used to moving around your groups checking on their needs say at five minute intervals, whatever the activity, then keeping an eye on the LOGO work fits into that pattern naturally. I don't have a five minute rule or anything: it is part of my natural teaching approach to pop back for a couple of minutes every five minutes or so.'

## Starting LOGO work in a school

*How would you get LOGO going in a school or encourage it to spread?*

'It's very hard to do it on your own. I think you need what we as a Project were lucky to have, somewhere to build a set of resources for teachers to help them and if possible someone for the teacher to talk to. Most of the teachers we've worked with on the Project had extensive experience with Turtle graphics before they introduced it in the classroom, and lots of support.

I think it is important for teachers to get to grips with LOGO. We have to accept that computers are becoming more and more important in our society. We certainly want to have available to us in primary schools resources which help us to interact on equal terms with our children instead of the initiative always coming from the teacher. So many of our materials don't allow for that.'

# 8 TURTLING WITH LOWER JUNIORS

Mrs Beryl Dobney has had many years' experience teaching lower juniors at Ickleford Primary School. There are 22 boys and only nine girls in the class.

On the day of my visit her class was working at tables in groups on a topic about transport. There was a happy atmosphere of quiet talk. Most of the children were using a well-known series of history books to collect information about roads and public transport through the ages, which they were putting into folders.

## Activities about transport using the floor Turtle

There was a large display on the wall entitled *Turtle City*, consisting mainly of pictures of vehicles which had been drawn out with a floor Turtle. This project had arisen from the term's topic. Among the items in Turtle City I spotted a rainbow and some stars, the word *Liverpool*, a tank, lorries, robots, jets and aeroplanes.

This class had had the use of a floor Turtle for a term before they came to Mrs Dobney.

### An aeroplane

In a corner of the room two children were using an Apple computer and floor Turtle for a program in which three triangles were being combined to make an aeroplane.

'We are using the small triangle for the front, big ones for the wings, then another small one for the back.'

They were able to explain how they used the same basic procedure for each set of triangles, changing the length of the side but keeping the angle of turn 120° in each case.

### A tank

Later some boys explained what they were doing: 'We made that tank and used a few small circles and a triangle. It nearly worked out except for the wheels which were a bit sort of messy and some were bigger than others. We couldn't do much about that so we left it.'

## Other activities

### A bird's nest

A problem arose when a group of boys, as part of their bird topic, decided to draw a nine-sided figure to represent a nest. They only managed to get half of the shape drawn out and then by repeating it were able to produce some sort of outline. Mrs Dobney suggested that they try to produce one complete shape. They used a calculator to divide 360 by 9 and having got the correct angle from that were able to write a procedure which drew out the correct shape.

### A flower

Some girls used hexagons to make a flower. They had seen an idea for using a ring of circles for a flower head in a LOGO booklet for teachers produced by the Chiltern Project team. One of the group 'dreamed up the idea' of the first hexagon while she was in bed. The group adapted the flower pattern to make their hexagon flower.

## Integrating LOGO into a fairly formal classroom

Mrs Dobney's class is run on a fairly formal, timetabled basis. The children are grouped by ability, but all work on the same subject at the same time.

*How did you integrate LOGO into your classroom?*

'I had had no experience till I started with the children, but last year I worked with the present 'J2' class and we had the computer for a term-and-a-half. This year I have started again.

We have a very flexible day in the first year juniors and even before we had the Turtle I was very well aware of what it was going to be like. I did a lot of preparatory work with the children: in movement lessons — turning and walking forward to make different shapes, walking around different shapes on the floor and so on.

We brought the Turtle in without the pen and guided it round a lot of obstacles which they had walked round themselves.

I think Katrina Blythe, our head, had discussed with us how we might make a start. But whenever I introduce angles to first year juniors I find that it's essential to walk it through, with their own bodies turning to the left and right before I do any formal work at all, so this is really where the idea came from.

By the time we put the pen in they were becoming a little more familiar with the computer keyboard. They worked very hard and managed to make all sorts of peculiar shapes. Some went right and some went wrong, but this was all free play without preplanning.

Next I began to plan by giving them half a shape and asking them to add the other half to produce a symmetrical figure. Some found that very difficult. They gradually became more aware of how to control the pen though very often they would still order it to turn to the left, when they really should have gone the opposite way.'

## Effective group work with the Turtle

*How did you get groups out to take their turn at the computer without distracting everybody else?*

'Well at first we had screens right around them except for one tiny entrance. But gradually they have become more used to having the Turtle work going on and now it doesn't matter if there is screen up or not.

We are lucky to have the use of the Apple full time. In the beginning we had a timetabled rota, but gradually I have had to lengthen the time each group has, so the timing had to become much more flexible. I also found after a while that ability groups worked better than friendship ones because unless the children were fairly evenly matched in ability one tended to get left holding the cord.

Each group has roughly an hour a week now and as they are doing more complicated work they don't want to stop in the middle. They didn't seem to mind so much in the beginning when they were just doing simple shapes. Now they really want to complete something and see it through, so they get anything from half-an-hour to an hour, depending on what they're doing and the amount of concentration they can give to it.

Some of the class are still working in direct drive. Others have recently started to write procedures in this half-term and at first it was just sufficiently exciting to have done that. I suggested that they might like to use a shape they had made in a larger procedure so the Turtle would know exactly what to do to draw several circles at a time, for instance.

This was very exciting and as you may have noticed today, they are now able to make a procedure for a shape, then store it and put it into a complicated shape system to build up more complicated programs. Last week two girls were rotating a hexagon to make a flower shape. This week they were moving it along horizontally to make a caterpillar. I had suggested that a caterpillar might be a possibility with circles, but it was their own idea to do one with hexagons. Now they are working on a procedure to give it L-shaped legs.'

## The benefits of working with LOGO

*What do you think first year juniors get from working with LOGO?*

'I think it's absolutely endless. Certainly where the maths is concerned they learn a great deal about geometric shapes. In the past when I have introduced the concept of an angle to first year juniors they have found it very difficult to realise that it's a measurement of turn rather than a measurement of length. I think the Turtle has helped tremendously. Now they measure angles very competently, understand what a right angle is, and can measure an angle greater or less than 90° easily. They are quite happy with quarter turns and half turns and realise that they are 90° and 180°. The brighter ones are now beginning to look at angles on a protractor which is another spin-off from the Turtle.

I take it home and do a bit of preparation. And of course we've had Katrina, who has been most helpful with any problems. I've found I've enjoyed it and the children have enjoyed it, so we've gone along together.

It's no good pretending that there aren't some things which have to be changed. The timetable has to be altered a little to make room for the computer studies, but I think it's well worth while because of the spin-off in many areas, not just maths.

The children gain by having to find their way around something completely fresh to them and when they have spotted something wrong and put it right, it increases their confidence right across the board.

Building up a program of their own is something positive. They have an incentive to learn how to cope with the language because it allows them to make things happen.

They are certainly drawing differently. The design aspect of art has come through much more because Turtle graphics are so strongly linked to art and to design which means they can see more clearly the basic structure of things instead of just making a pretty picture.

I think their factual writing has become more concise because if they have had to write about a particular procedure they've put in they've had to think and write in a different, more precise way than is usual for that age group.'

*What about social development?*

'I still have one boy whom I find it difficult to integrate into a group at all. He's very bright and will take over whichever group he is in and monopolise a situation. He is also inclined to say, 'That's my copyright and no one else must touch it', which is rather a nice idea! It shows he's very egocentric still but it's helped the others to work together.'

*Have you noticed any differences between girls and boys?*

'The girls tend to want to produce flowers and gardens and butterflies. The boys are much more orientated towards cars and jeeps. But on the other hand as they have become more used to using the Turtle they are all tending to move towards abstract shapes rather than pictures. So the boys and girls are beginning to do similar things.

At first they are overawed by the floor Turtle: it's not quite alive, yet it does all these wonderful things that they tell it to do. Now some of them are beginning to ask if they can just use the screen because it's so much faster than the floor Turtle.

The brighter ones make the transition perfectly happily because the speed is important to them. The slower ones feel the need to see the lines being drawn out so they can orientate their own body with the Turtle. They still have to put their right hand out before they can instruct the Turtle to turn.'

*I notice they use planning books. How did that arise?*

'At first we were writing the plans on paper and pinning them to the drawings made with the floor Turtle. If it didn't come off it didn't matter too much because we would just discard it and try again. But they began to want to keep things, and as they got more and more procedures they wanted to keep track of what they had made. Some of them now have as many as 14 procedures on their file. The books are an additional, permanent record.

Usually they share what they find. When they first made circles a lot of discussion went on which I think is good. We often have a discussion about what we have made that week and how we came to design a particular shape. I think it helps them all.

We had a boy go home yesterday who had been trying to make an octagon. He had had several failures during the day and had gone home and asked his dad, who told him exactly what to do. Luckily by the time he got back to school he'd forgotten again, so he had to do it for himself. It is so important that they learn from their own mistakes. That is one of the main points of LOGO.

I must admit that I was very wary at first about introducing LOGO because I felt it was going to interrupt the children's basic skills lessons. But after I took the computer home and tried it out for myself I realised that it was going to help the children in many more ways than merely being able to type a few words into a machine. I've tried to keep one step ahead of them by taking it home to prepare, and it's been well worth the effort.'

# 9 IN AT THE DEEP END

Austin Cheminais and Sara James team teach parallel classes of eight to nine year olds at Delves Junior School. One of the fourth year classes at Delves is involved in the Walsall LOGO Project and a group of children from the third year are withdrawn once a week to work with the Project coordinator, Julian Pixton, who also helps the Project class.

The staff at Delves have a small amount of inservice training, mostly lunchtime sessions run by Julian Pixton and the LOGO group's class teacher, Janice Staines, whose work is described in another chapter.

Mr Cheminais' and Miss James' experiences while getting started, plunging almost unaided in at the deep end with LOGO, may be of particular interest to teachers who find themselves beginning LOGO work without much in the way of training or specialist help.

## The teachers' early work with LOGO

*When did you first use LOGO?*

Mr Cheminais: 'We began using LOGO in September 1984. We have 43 children between us and share one BBC computer, which is available to use every day except Wednesday.'

Miss James: 'We started without a Turtle so the children were drawing on the screen, but all of them had had experience with Big Trak. However, the floor Turtle was quickly reintroduced because we felt the children needed a more concrete experience.'

*How did the computer and LOGO fit into your organisation?*

Mr Cheminais: 'Julian Pixton took a group consisting of about a third of the year altogether, so we tried to introduce the rest of the year to LOGO.'

Miss James: 'Once we knew we had exclusive use of one computer we grouped the children into pairs. We decided that the children should work for two half-hour sessions a week and planned a LOGO timetable.'

Mr Cheminais: 'To avoid the possibility of the children working on LOGO at the expense of other areas of the curriculum we spread the rota over two weeks, so that the children would be working on the computer at a different time each week.'

# Problems — and their solutions

*What problems did you have to start with?*

Mr Cheminais: 'We were initially faced with quite a few organisational problems. The LOGO timetable proved to be too inflexible. It didn't allow for sessions missed because of visitors, the machine breaking down, or the computer being in use elsewhere. So the rota never really worked properly.'

Miss James: 'The pairs in Julian Pixton's group who were using the screen Turtle and saving their programs on disks were interspersed amongst the other pairs on the rota who were using the floor Turtle. This meant that we had to keep changing the computer from disk drive to floor Turtle and vice versa.'

Mr Cheminais: 'The hardware was unfamiliar to use, so we might spend five, ten, or even twenty minutes trying to find out why the computer wasn't working, only to find that you hadn't got the wretched junction in properly. Having to load up disks for some pairs, but not others, was also time consuming, and sometimes disks got wiped accidentally.'

Miss James: 'During the autumn term we became concerned because, having introduced the hardware and overcoming some of the problems we had had with organisation, the children seemed to be making very little progress.'

Mr Cheminais: 'We could see that the Project group was progressing but the children we had weren't getting anywhere because we couldn't give them enough time. The two children on the computer had to compete with the other children in the class for our attention.'

Miss James: 'They tended to keep coming up to us every time they met a problem while we were working with other children and there would be nothing we could do about it at that point. The children in the Project group tended to be the more able ones and they had the advantage of an hour a week of extra tuition, so if they made mistakes they could rectify them.

For the average children, unless someone was there to put the right question at the right time, not telling them, but just helping them to trace their errors in a constructive way and encouraging them to order their thoughts with questions like, 'What do you think would happen if you went there?', they could just be flailing around on the keyboard for half-an-hour and achieving very little.

The pairs who were using the floor Turtle were playing games (on the advice of experts) which we found confusing. They seemed to be just messing about and we couldn't tell whether they were just playing or whether they were learning something useful.

Someone would be sitting at the keyboard trying to get the Turtle to move, or they might be estimating the distance it needed to travel, or how far it would need to go to knock a skittle over, but we didn't understand why or what the games were. Some would be playing one game and some another.'

Mr Cheminais: 'We weren't sure how useful these games were with the groups we had. Julian Pixton was doing similar things with his group, but he had the time to sit with them and see what they were learning from this sort of activity. We didn't.'

*How did you overcome these problems?*

Mr Cheminais: 'We decided to stop working with LOGO for a while. We taped some games which were written in BASIC and the children who weren't going to Julian Pixton played them as a way of becoming familiar with the keyboard and the screen. It was a stop-gap to give us time to take stock and define more precisely the direction in which the pupils should be heading and the steps which should be taken to achieve this.

We also found that the children benefited — especially the quieter ones — from playing games as they became more accustomed to using the keyboard.'

Miss James: 'It also gave us time to go away, have some lunchtime sessions with Julian Pixton and Janice Staines in which we were able to play with the Turtle ourselves. These sessions gave us a clearer idea of the steps through which the pupils should be progressing. We decided to start everybody off drawing with the Turtle and to build up gradually to making programs.'

Mr Cheminais: 'We made two changes in the way we organised things; one to do with planning and the other starting what we call the LOGO session. One session from the rota was allocated to a group discussion round the computer about any problems that the children had encountered during the week. Ways of solving problems were proffered by the pupils themselves. Julian's group with their greater experience of the computer made valuable contributions for these discussions. The children had to plan what they were going to draw with the Turtle before they got to the computer. They did this by drawing a picture and then writing out the commands they thought were necessary in order to achieve this. They then tested it out at the keyboard and tried to correct any errors.

There was a bit of disagreement at first over how far the children should be guided in what they drew. Initially we wanted to have a list of very simple shapes — oblongs, squares, and triangles — and get them to go away, plan those and then draw them, as the first stage.

Julian Pixton said that deciding their own goal was part of the process and so was failing and going through the process of correcting mistakes.'

Miss James: 'So we just limited ourselves to saying, 'Choose a simple picture to draw', but it became very difficult when some of them came up with very complex pictures to which our reaction was: 'How are they going to get anywhere with this?' We then, by careful questioning, tried to direct the children towards a simpler task.

When we introduced the LOGO session the children were familiar with putting **FD** for **FORWARD** and so on. Many wrote down an estimate of what they thought they would do, then in the group session we would go over one person's plan. We would discuss what they intended to do, and what they would need to do if it went wrong (change it and try again). Julian had said that that was how he wanted us to do it, so at least we now had more confidence in ourselves and what we were trying to achieve.

A lot of discussion work came out of the group sessions and in fact working as a group proved to be better for the pairs as well as the class as a whole.

I asked how far they thought it actually should be. It was certainly far easier for them to estimate the correct length when they could actually see the red line or the green line drawn which they knew was 450.

'Well, let's put it back and halve it' they'd say, and 'Let's put 200.' We changed it and wrote down the new number on the board. A lot of discussion work came out of that and in fact working as a group proved to be better for the pairs as well as the class as a whole.

Now that they are used to planning we are getting on much more efficiently all round. If they hit a snag, or get stuck we can say, 'Bring me a plan. Which command was it? Well what do you think you ought to do next?' They've got something themselves to refer to, and after consulting you briefly, they can go back, change it and try again.

We usually make sure they have a task or a job to work on the following week, either on or off the machine.'

Mr Cheminais: 'Mark you, we have small classes this year but next year we'll have another 20 children and only one computer, so our current organisation won't necessarily be appropriate.'

## The teachers' previous experience with computers

*I asked about their own training.*

Mr Cheminais: 'I had used a Tandy computer before I came here, but really as a sort of glorified work sheet with prerecorded programs, simple maths and reading exercises and so on.'

Miss James: 'I had negligible experience with computers. Listening to enthusiasts expound upon the marvellous capability of the computer had made me apprehensive of using a machine myself.'

Mr Cheminais: 'Last year we mainly observed LOGO from afar. As the Project was in its infancy and the class I was working with were using Big Trak, that tended to be the area upon which attention was focussed.'

Miss James: 'We both took home the micro with the Turtle chip and tried to do something with it, but found the instruction booklet completely confusing. It would have been useful to have had access to someone like Mr Pixton or an experienced teacher, just to show us what to do.'

Mr Cheminais: 'We both would have welcomed some sort of practical workshop course with the Turtle before we started using it, rather than afterwards.

A course like that is most useful when started at the very simplest level. There's an assumption, which is made by people with an expertise in anything, that you know a little, so the instruction doesn't start early enough.

For example, when I took the computer home I took out all the bits, hooked it all in and couldn't get the thing to work at all, I had to phone somebody up and it turned out that all that had happened was that I had failed to press the right key.

Perhaps a long course would have helped or even one lasting six or eight weeks when we started off, with a follow-up course the next term to introduce the next stage or whatever.'

Miss James: 'Among the lessons we've learned is how useful it would have been to have had access to several machines instead of just the one, and to have had a Turtle full time.

We have also realised learning with the children makes it harder, but it's not impossible, and that having a bit of time at lunchtimes to play on your own can be a great help. However, it is important to have someone you can refer to while you are learning.'

## The dangers of evangelising about LOGO

Both teachers had a number of reservations about the claims made for LOGO as a unique way of working with children.

Mr Cheminais: 'Working with LOGO has helped improve the skills of working together, planning and discussion. But we've done other things besides LOGO to stimulate group discussion. It's become part of an overall strategy.'

Miss James: 'People can become very missionary about LOGO and give what is perhaps an exaggerated place to computers.

It is valuable for problem solving and pupils do get to develop all sorts of skills that they wouldn't perhaps normally exercise an awful lot in the rest of the curriculum.

There are other areas of the curriculum through which you can develop these skills. For example, in science the teacher tends to ask questions like, 'What can you see? What does this tell you?' which are exactly the same sorts of questions that you can ask when you are using LOGO at a computer. And this also applies to language, maths, topic. It is not unique to LOGO.

One of LOGO's real values is in helping pupils to cope with failure. If they try out a program and it goes wrong you can encourage them to think about how to put it right. They are put in a situation where failure is creative, where they can actually do something about mistakes.

Since they usually do succeed in correcting bugs, they come to look on mistakes as an enjoyable challenge. I think its probably true that you can set up that sort of learning situation more easily with LOGO than other things.'

Mr Cheminais: 'I think the opportunity for forward planning is also something which LOGO provides better than most other activities can.

We have acquired a certain level of knowledge now, but I imagine that we'll continue to come across the same problems as our children progress. Where next, if you like.'

Miss James: 'One point was raised about the value of encouraging children to draw shapes on a screen which were supposed to be cars or boats or whatever, but which don't resemble the way those things look in reality at all. Most of the time we say, 'Draw what you see'. Yet when using the computer we expect children to simplify the pictures that they draw.'

Mr Cheminais: 'We also feel that perhaps the claims made linking maths and LOGO might be exaggerated. To be fair I have found that as well as being more expert with the machine Julian Pixton's group have been able to make those sort of links much more readily, perhaps because they have been able to spend more time working with the Turtle.'

Miss James: 'I think it is important for teachers to realise that LOGO exists. In some schools computers lie around unused, except perhaps by one enthusiast. Or they are used with commercial or home-made drill and practice programs only. Many teachers are unaware of the true potential of computers.'

Mr Cheminais: 'I think too, that if all we wanted was for the children to be able to draw a square or a hexagon by the end of the year, we could achieve that very easily.

I would like them to be on the way to being able to do more than that. What's important is being able to ask them to produce a square or a house and for them to say, 'Fine', and be able to work out how to do it by themselves after say 20 minutes at the machine. It's the process that is important.'

# State of the art

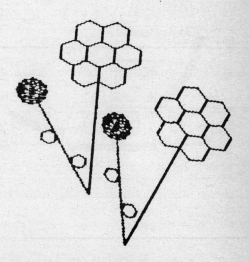

*See page 196 for the program to produce these flowers.*

# 10 USING A NETWORK

The staff and children at Ickleford Primary School had been using LOGO for about a year when the school was offered the use of a computer network.

Six RML microcomputers with individual monitors linked to a network server were installed in a spacious Victorian classroom with high ceilings and large windows set high up in the brick walls. Instead of keeping their files on disks which they fed into individual disk drives beside their computers, the children's files would be placed on one disk held centrally by the network server.

The advantage of this system is, apparently, that with the number of files stored in this way, though each pair of children works at a separate keyboard and screen, they can call up and use not only their own files but anyone else's stored on the same disk.

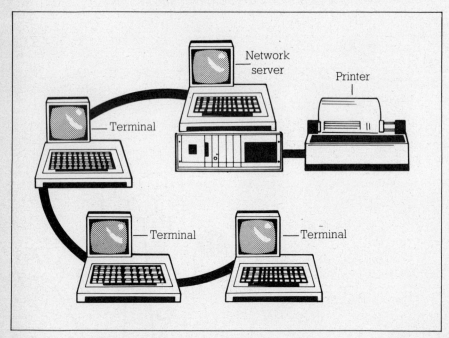

*A plan of a typical microcomputer network.*

# The network in use at Ickleford

Each class has access to the network twice a week. The whole class moves into the computer room for half a day. While one group of twelve works at the machines the rest sit at tables nearby, planning their next job for the computer, or doing some related work in mathematics, their current topic, or art.

At the time of my visit these children had been working with LOGO for about five terms, first with a floor Turtle and then on the screen. Katrina Blythe, their headteacher, had replaced Richard Noss as the Chiltern LOGO Project coordinator, and was spending the morning with the class as consultant to the children and their teacher.

On the wall was a frieze entitled *Apple World*, made the previous year when the class topic had been space. It depicts an alien world peopled by mechanical creatures controlled by computers. The creatures, drawn out on a floor Turtle, had been pinned up with the following story by Alexandra, aged eight:

# A story by Alexandra

- Unknown in the darkness and gloom was a dismal, grey planet. The meaning of this planet was not known. Until an astronaut came out of the solar system and got lost in the gloom. As he was giving up all hope he hit something solid. He wasn't sure whether it was solid, because when he looked out of the window he saw his rocket was slowly sinking. He had to think quickly, so he got out as fast as he could. When he got out he noticed there was a crowd of mechanical creatures.

  There was a cat with gleaming eyes, a spider with its spindly legs. There was a robot being programmed by some little Turtles. Each Turtle was scurrying around doing their jobs. There were also some flowers scattered around. Each one looked just like a miniature stained glass window.

  The astronaut was just about to ask them what the planet was when there was an explosion. One of the Turtles rushed the astronaut to safety. The Turtle explained that every now and then they had a volcanic explosion. The astronaut said 'I've got some chemicals in my rocket that will cure those explosions.' He went back to the rocket and got the chemicals. As the astronaut could not get back to his own solar system he decided to live in Apple World.

## The morning class using the network

David Cripps's class used the network for the first part of the day. Their project this term is the weather and he had asked each group to use their computer time to come up with something connected with that topic. A number of the groups waiting for their turn were planning what they would draw when the computer was available.

I spoke to some of them:

'What I like about LOGO is the fact that you can build what you want.'

'I like it when you can get to the part where you can just get on with what you want to make. At home people just play games with computers which is not what they are meant for. They are for working. I've learnt to concentrate more on my other work because on the computer you have to concentrate on what you're doing.'

'I'm not a very good drawer. LOGO helps you with maths and it helps you to draw. It's easier to rub out on the screen than with a pencil because when you use a rubber it leaves little lines. If you make a mistake on the screen you can delete it.'

*A network in use in a classroom.*

Other children said that working with LOGO is 'adventurous' and that they enjoy the fact that 'you can make your own things'.

I suggested that this was surely just as true of working with say, LEGO or paint.

'Yes but this is more exciting and on LEGO you can lose parts, but on this you don't.'

'So far we have drawn dogs, a snowman and a television and now we are planning a rain gauge. Our program is too long so we have to break it into smaller procedures, otherwise it will use up too much of the memory.'

Some like working alone, but others enjoy having a partner to help work things out. I asked some of the teams at the screen what they were doing.

'We are trying to make a house. It keeps going upside down but we like it when it's hard. Our robot and glasses were hard. We have learned to label so we will be able to put **THIS IS OUR SNOWMAN VILLAGE** at the top of this scene when we have finished it.'

Two girls had drawn a rain cloud.

'We prepared a curve on paper, but it wasn't quite right so we were told to fiddle around on the computer till we got it. Now it's about right.'

## The differences between DART and LOGO

Mr Cripps had worked with DART at another school, but this is his first year using full LOGO.

*What had he found to be the major differences?*

'The children can make much more elaborate procedures with LOGO. They can add instructions together in a more comprehensive way which enables them to see a sequence of events more clearly. The list-processing facility allows them to make use of written language and combine words with numbers on the screen, which you can't do with DART.

One boy is using an if/then program which is like conventional computer programming, but he is using it in a very personal, relevant way.

RML LOGO's *label* facility allows the children to alternate between pictures and writing in a very natural way. They can illustrate their poem or story as they go along or add graphics to words. It's more versatile than a word-processing package because you can draw on the screen at the same time as you are writing. The words can come up inside the pictures or be added at any stage.'

Two boys have used this label facility to draw an umbrella and some rain. They then wrote **RAIN, RAIN GO AWAY COME AGAIN ANOTHER DAY** under the picture.

## The afternoon class using the network

Ellen Tuck's fourth year junior class moved into the room to use the network later in the day. She described the stages through which they had moved to get to their present levels.

'At the beginning of September the procedures they could build were basic geometric shapes. They began to rotate them, then to translate them into other shapes and finally into patterns built up from sets of shapes. Now they are all at very different stages.'

One boy was working in direct drive, trying to draw an illuminated T in 'old-fashioned script'. He had got the idea from an old Bible.

Two girls were trying to find the bug in their BLAST-OFF program.

'We started off just trying to build a rocket then we decided to have it going into space. We were having a few problems with the countdown which printed out the words **10 9 8 7 6 5 4 3 2 1 WE HAVE A LIFT-OFF**, so we decided to make it shorter by using a list, but something has obviously gone wrong.

We put **LIST [10 9 8 7 6 5 4 3 2 1 0 BLAST OFF]** down, but instead of the rocket showing on the screen during the countdown, it has vanished altogether.

It's putting in this new procedure called **LIST** that's mucked it up. When we have sorted the bug out we are going to have half the rocket going up the screen so it looks as if it's moving. Then we'll have a report from space and at the end we are planning to do the bit where the nose-cone lands in the sea and there will be a splash.'

The girls worked away at the problem unaided for some considerable time. Katrina Blythe kept an eye on them but decided not to intervene for the moment. They were checking each procedure in turn and eventually decided that the bug was probably in the procedure called **LIFT** at the point where it said **BD (BACKWARD) 50** and **DROP**.

I asked whether they were finding the process frustrating.

'I think it's nice to have a problem. It's interesting because it gives you something to work on.'

The list-processing facility of LOGO allows a series of commands to be written within brackets. The children can instruct the computer to select items from the list and use them in a variety of ways, on their own or with graphics. Lists can be made of numbers, letters, words or notes of music.

(In music, the length and volume of notes can be varied by combining a note, say E, from the first list, with a duration of five, available in a second list and a volume of nine, which is contained in a third list, and so on. Examples of children using this facility are given in the section on Delves Junior School, Walsall, on page 121.)

## Using a list procedure to draw a snail called Fred

Two children showed me their program SNAIL which illustrates how this facility can respond to the primary child's imagination. Though these children do not have access to Sprites they produce animations by drawing out shapes then erasing them and redrawing them elsewhere.

A spiral snail shell is traced out, then the body is drawn, followed by some flowers (hexagons on stalks). The snail produces two feelers, one of which is gradually extended until it touches the flowers. Part of one flower is erased or *eaten* then the following words appear as a caption — **YUM YUM VERY TASTY**.

The children explained how SNAIL had developed:

'The idea of drawing hexagons came from an art lesson about shapes. We worked out how to draw a hexagon spiral then stopped it at a certain place to draw its shell and then made his body. We had a few problems as we were going along. We put **SET X 200** to move it across the screen, but the body stayed behind and only the shell moved. Mrs Blythe had to help us.'

'We used **LABEL** then typed in the message to add the words. Now we are trying to make the feelers on our snail grow so it will touch the flower. We like watching the mistakes. It's fun.'

## A more detailed explanation

Katrina Blythe explained the development of SNAIL in greater detail to illustrate some of the potential of LOGO.

'It started with a class project about structures and these two children decided to investigate hexagons.

Initially they wrote a program to draw a hexagon which could be of any size. To do that they had to learn how to handle variables. They then proceeded to put in a variety of inputs which built it into a lovely pattern.

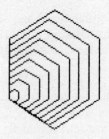

Next they went back to the original idea, but using much tinier inputs which they linked to make a more complex pattern.

The third variation uses one hexagon rotated a number of times around a fixed point which was later used as the basis for the flowers.

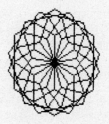

So, having worked out a basic shape they played with it in free exploration.

Then they came and said they would very much like to make the hexagon grow and they didn't know how to do that. I had to give them a procedure which drew a hexagon whose side grew by ten each time it was drawn out.

They went off to explore this program. At first they made all the shapes grow by ten but varied the starting size. When that became too limiting they wanted it to grow by five each time, which condensed the whole shape.

As they became more confident they wanted to make the growing amount a variable too. So, entirely on their own they wrote a program to draw a spiralling hexagon, which can start off at any size and increase by any amount they put in.

I don't think that teachers need to feel diffident about giving children a technique sometimes because they will take it off, explore it and then completely convert it into something of their own.

It's very common for children to take one very simple idea and explore it as far as they can, then to decide that they can do something quite specific with it. This case is typical, for having got this far they decided to use the spiral to draw the shell of a snail called Fred.

His body was made by exploring and working out angles and lengths and there's a little circle for his head. But it's the shell that they were clearly interested in.

However, if you try to use a spiralling procedure within another one you come up against a problem. Their original procedure was a recursive one. The children think of that as meaning that the program keeps on calling up a copy of itself into which they can put different variables. In this case the spiral is growing with an extra input and goes on for ever unless they put in a conditional line to stop it.

They, therefore, had to learn to put in a conditional statement. They decided to command the spiral to stop when the length of a side became greater than 34.

Then they decided to spin their original hexagon to make a flower. Because the first one they made was too big for the snail they had to make another to the right scale.

At this point they went through their procedures tidying them up. If they'd got something like **RIGHT 40** followed by **LEFT 90**, put in while they were exploring originally in direct drive, they would say, 'Well that really is the same as **LEFT 50**' and so on, tidying up their thinking.

The fun really started as they tried to move their snail across the screen. When they moved the starting point across the screen and asked the Turtle to draw the snail in the new position, the shell was drawn there but the body stayed behind, and was drawn out in the original position.

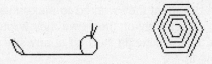

*Fred the snail — the shell was drawn in the new position but the body stayed behind.*

They thought this was very very funny. The fact that it wasn't what they wanted didn't matter at all and they explored this idea, leaving the shell right at the edge of the screen and the body further along. Eventually they drew two shells on either side of the screen, popped the snail in the middle and called it *Moving House*. They were so pleased with it that they put their names — Roderic and Jenny — at the bottom on the print-out.

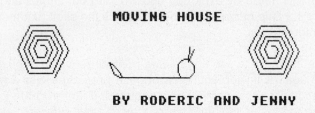

*The children's imaginative solution to their problem.*

Now while they were doing this they realised what the bug was, but they felt it was so much fun exploring it that they didn't want to put it right at that point. In actual fact in their original procedure they had used coordinates so that the shell would be drawn wherever the Turtle was. Then they had something called **SET X 200**, which moves the Turtle to a particular point on the screen to draw the rest of the snail. But whenever they moved the Turtle to a particular point to start the drawing off, it would draw the shell but would go back to **SET X 200** to draw the body.

They had to go through a laborious business to get the Turtle to the right place to draw the body where they wanted it. The method they used was less neat than **SET X**, but more suitable for animation. They were very meticulous and took about four hours altogether, but they were determined to end up with a product which matched the idea they had very firmly in their minds.

Finally, the snail starts off at one side of the screen, he is rubbed out and reappears closer to the flowers. One of his antennae touches the flowers and one of the flowers is erased to show that it has been eaten. Then the words **YUM YUM VERY TASTY** come up.

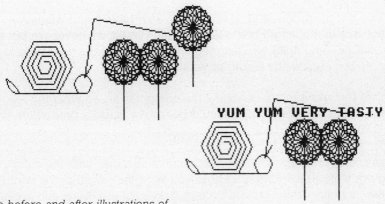

*The before and after illustrations of*
*Fred the snail eating one of the flowers.*

This is a good example of how children are prepared to explore one simple idea and using the flexibility of LOGO take it as far as they are capable at that point. It also shows that children aren't worried by their mistakes. Too often, I think, children's learning is held back by a fear of making mistakes. They have a picture of learning as being either right or wrong, whereas when you start to try and program a computer you seldom get it right. It's only as you become more skilled that you are able to spot bugs and put them right quickly. So LOGO helps eliminate this very clear-cut distinction between right and wrong.

SNAIL is also a good example of how a mistake can be creative and act as a lateral way of developing a new idea or variation on an idea. I think the marked persistence children exhibit arises because the problem is their own. No one else has set it. They have decided what they wanted to do and they are, therefore, motivated to persist till it is achieved.'

## Other work arising from Fred the snail

'The other thing the SNAIL example shows is the great wealth of problem solving and variety of approaches that can spring from investigating and modifying one idea.'

### An interactive mathematics game

Two girls showed me an interactive program which they had designed. It began with the drawing of a simple rectangle, which they built up into a complex pattern. Then they wanted to be able to vary the length and width of the rectangle.

'We wrote a procedure RECT, LENGTH, WIDTH, with FORWARD and whatever amount was in the length box, RIGHT 90, then FORWARD whatever we put in the width box and RIGHT 90. This meant that we could get the Turtle to draw out rectangles any length or width we chose.

Then we thought it might be nice if the computer asked what the length and the width of the rectangle should be, so we made a procedure called RECT2 which did this.'

The resulting program is a sort of mathematics game, with the computer doing the work. It asks what number you want the length or the width to be, then not only draws out the correct shape but also gives the area of that particular rectangle, even if fairly complicated numbers like 2.53 are used. The girls were proud to have made something which they and their friends could use to help find the answers to the sort of problem they might come up against in a mathematics book.

### A procedure named WHOOPS

While I was there the boy and girl on SNAIL began experimenting with a pattern of concentric semicircles and discovered by accident that if they typed in a minus number they would produce a mirror image of the original shapes. They then began to explore the different shapes which were produced by varying the minus numbers. They tentatively named the procedure WHOOPS!

## Complex patterns

Two boys have been working on elaborate patterns for several weeks. They produced a series of beautiful triangles, squares and hexagons, and superimposed them all on the screen for the first time while I watched. Clearly the mathematics they were using to produce these shapes was less important to them than the unexpected and very attractive patterns that were being drawn out.

# Talking with the class teacher

Ellen Tuck described how she started working with LOGO:

'I began with a class of second year juniors in October 1983. We had a computer and a floor Turtle which we shared with another class so we had the use of it about half the day.

We based our groups on mathematical ability. At first we had teams of fours, but we soon found that this left one person with nothing to do, so we rearranged them into threes. That turned out to be the best size for a team. One had to hold the Turtle's lead to stop it getting tangled up, one did the typing and the third would read off from their plans.

At first they just experimented, drawing whatever they liked to find out what the Turtle could do. They liked 90° to begin with. That was a familiar angle, they knew what it would do, and they preferred to turn right because as the majority of them are right-handed, it is very much a dominant direction.

We started off with obstacle courses on the floor. They had to manoeuvre the Turtle round skittles by typing in commands on the keyboard which would send it round the course and back to a base.

From there we developed more intricate kinds of courses on the floor drawn out on paper which they had to follow.

We tried to move them away from 90°, to explore other possible ways of turning. The children at first homed in on numbers they knew, like 50 or 100. If they were aiming for a target they would creep up, inching towards it adding a little bit on at a time to get there. As time went by and they began to get some sense of what distance the Turtle units would cover they became much more accurate, and found it easier to approximate and estimate length and distance.

The first thing they all wanted to draw was a square. They didn't seem to think at first that there were other shapes they could draw. They all liked a square or a rectangle.

Then we began working on a topic about space. And without my suggesting it at all the children began to explore the idea of making space ships. Well of course this meant that they had to find out how to use angles of different sizes, not just 90°. They tended to avoid circles because they couldn't work out how to draw a curve. Instead they went on to triangles.

There was a tremendous amount of excited chit-chat outside the classroom, during playtimes and lunchtimes. I noticed that once one group had found out something, in no time at all they'd all be trying it.'

## From the floor to the screen Turtle

'For many the transition to the screen caused a regression in their work because the scale of the Turtle units was so different. But like everything else with children once they'd had some practice it was all right.

I started them off with some exercises in symmetry. On an acetate I would draw half a shape and they would draw the other half. Once they began to draw their own shapes they kept to things they knew, building up simple shapes which changed into more complex ones, rotating one shape into a pattern and so on.

The most interesting thing I've found is that because screen drawings can be erased children do not have this problem of worrying about making a mistake at all. They feel completely free to explore as much as they want to without having to face a picture that says, 'Oh, I've done that wrong'. They know that they can always start again.

Working with LOGO on the computer seems to give them a freedom which they don't have even when they are drawing, writing or painting.

## I foresaw many problems when I started

'I'm very enthusiastic about working with computers now. Though I came to it with an open mind I could foresee all sorts of problems to do with classroom organisation. Was it going to be a distraction in my classroom? Would the children be drawn away from their other work when someone was working on the computer? How was I going to be able to record what one group was doing on the computer while other children did other work? Those sorts of things.

As my class has always worked in groups anyway, after watching for a week, the children accepted the computer and got on with their own work. They knew that their time would come round and were content with that arrangement.

I think that planning is vital. The children soon come to realise that their time on the computer is short so to make the best use of it they have a period before their 40 minutes on the machine planning the work for that day and a period afterwards to work out what they will do the following week.

I insist that in addition to planning out the commands they write out in words a description of what they will be trying to do at the computer. It helps them to order their thoughts and gives them extra time to think about exactly how they are going to achieve what they have in mind.'

## LOGO succeeds with a wide range of abilities

I remarked on how confident and articulate the children seemed as they explained their work to me.

*What have you found most useful about working with LOGO?*

'One of the most valuable things is that LOGO offers something to all ability levels. My less able children have gained a great deal of confidence not just with numbers but generally. They don't hesitate now to make suggestions or to try things out.

For example, two of those boys you were talking to earlier, whom you thought were among my most able, both have IQs in the 90s. One of them in particular is very diffident about his maths. He often makes problems for himself over number work which partly stem from insecurity and lack of confidence. But when he works on the computer he doesn't spend time worrying about whether something is going to work for him this time. He just plunges right in and attempts things which in other areas of maths he finds much more difficult to do.'

*I commented on the fact that several pairs consisted of a boy and a girl and asked who decided on the combinations.*

'Oh, I decide that. I move the partners around. I think putting them into mathematical pairings was a very useful way to begin with. But it's like every other subject. It doesn't always follow that the children's progress will stay uniform within one group, therefore you have to be very flexible and say that if one partner could go much further than the other she may have to be moved and swap around as the need arises.

I haven't seen any evidence that boys and girls use it differently. I would say that ability is what counts. Able girls make as much progress as the boys. They may not wish to talk about what they are doing as much as the boys. Boys are much more vocal. They love to explain everything to everyone in the class, to make sure that everyone knows, but the girls, who may be at exactly the same stage, tend to be quieter. It may be that at this age the girls are more mature. But they progress just the same.'

## Some further experiences

'At first, though a lot of the work was exploratory, I had to teach individual pairs how to build up procedures, and edit, etc. Now that they are more experienced my role is to step in from time to time when they come to the inevitable plateaux.

When a child makes up something that works it's a lovely experience for them and often they would quite happily stay at that stage, reinforcing the satisfaction. But you can't afford to allow time for too much of that. They learn more if they are exposed to new ideas. So at that point I suggest some new avenues for them to explore. I just pose a question and leave them to investigate it.

One of the interesting things, to me, is the way they all manage to concentrate when they work with LOGO, even the children who find it hard to do that with other work. It arouses a great deal of interest from every child in the class, which is very unusual. They have been used to computers for a very long time now but their interest hasn't dwindled. It seems to have settled into a very positive enthusiasm which has continued for all the children.

I think one has to be careful that they do not fail too often. It is important to step in if a child continues to fail at something they have set themselves to do. I think that if you let them struggle on for too long you probably would begin to have children who would not want to do it any more.

I think it is important for teachers not to feel threatened by LOGO even though it is something new. At first I took the machine and manual home and just worked through it. It took me some time to become comfortable with it and in fact I am still learning, but I found it interesting to be in the same situation as the children. It helped me to see how they would feel and react and I think I was more sensitive to how they might approach it because I had recently been through the same experience.

As with the rest of the curriculum, I feel that if I am to be useful to the children I should try to stay a little ahead of them if I can. But at the same time this is an activity where children can go off at such tangents that they don't expect you always to be there before them. If I don't know the answer, then we try to work through it together. After all we are supposed to be exploring and investigating. But in the majority of cases it's a matter of my taking the machine home so that if anything crops up I will be able to give a hand.

One particular advantage of starting LOGO off fresh with junior-aged children is that it has given me an unusual chance to observe what happens when a child learns something from scratch. By this age, most of the time they are building on things they started learning as infants, be it drawing, writing, maths, etc. The basics are all in place. It's been very useful to see genuine new learning taking place.

I was a bit worried at first about the time factor. There is so much that we already have to fit in, but I have found that it links up with many areas of their work. We don't just use it for maths investigations. It depends what they're working on at the time. Some children use it in connection with their topic work, others art, or maths.

Some of them have found that they can make an image on the screen appear, disappear and reappear. Lots of them had been to see the film *Ghostbusters* and so they wanted to make their own ghostbusters.

Some of the older, more able ones use list processing, but basically they build shapes and patterns and develop the mathematical and imaginative work which comes from it. Accurate spelling is also important, though of course if they invent a title for a program that can be spelled any way they like. If they forget what the spelling of their program is the worst that can happen is a message on the screen saying LOGO CAN'T... whatever it is, which is valuable psychologically.

They see it as a natural way of expressing ideas, which is what one wants in a primary school and it builds up their fluency and confidence. I don't think LOGO interferes with other work. On the contrary it enhances it.'

## Some reflections

'As we have been going along we've reflected on what we've seen happening and we are beginning to have some idea of the stages a child will go through.

First they will explore freely, then they may start to see patterns within the things they have made. They may use those and develop ideas further. For a while they will stay on that level, while perhaps getting more divergent. Then something will happen which prompts another question and they will move to the next stage.

In the majority of cases the children dictate the speed at which they work. We have tried introducing something new to a child without them asking a question. The child will work with it for that lesson, but often they won't make it their own. They'll revert to what they want to do. Until they are ready to accept and understand they won't use anything you give them. They have to need it and make it their own.

If we lost the use of the computers and LOGO now I think my class would miss out on the chance to develop skills of investigation, and creating their own problems to solve, things we are trying to provide for all the time in our classsrooms. They now have the means to invent their own problems, instead of having to work on something introduced externally by teacher. Because the problem is theirs they have a strong motive for working out a solution. I also like the fact that it allows children to make mistakes which they don't see as a failure, but as an integral part of their learning. They use their mistakes in a positive way to develop their ideas.

It does a great deal for their logical thinking. One can see it in their science work, for instance, in the way they plan now. They have developed a set method of doing things, of following ideas through logically and also within that, being creative and divergent in their thinking. They will try out different methods, not always go along one path, because they see that in that way they may arrive at a better solution.

I would like to do some work with computers on making files and retrieving information, but I also plan to stick with LOGO. I wouldn't work without it now. I'm like the children. I get very excited when they have accomplished something they really want to do. It's wonderful.'

## Using LOGO on a network

The aim in introducing the network at Ickleford was to see what use, if any, children made of the facility it offered for looking and using each other's work. The Chiltern group wanted to get some idea of whether a network was a desirable way of using computers for LOGO.

I asked Katrina Blythe to comment on how it had been operating so far:

'At first we tried sending the third and fourth year children down in groups to use the network in the computer room, but by the end of the first term we had decided against that. LOGO was coming to be seen as something separate instead of forming part of the classroom activities, something within the curriculum which offered a chance for independent, conjectural learning to develop.

So now the whole class moves down to that area of the school for a morning and they combine the computer work with other activities. The children get a couple of sessions each per week and while this may mean that the computer network is lying empty some of the time at least when it is in use it is within a class context, which is vital. I don't feel guilty about not keeping it in constant use. You have to leave space for all the other parts of the primary curriculum as well.

The networking aspect hasn't really developed fully so far. Some of the children are still a bit confused by it. They found it a little remote. Interestingly, they can identify with a disk drive just in front of them as the place where their procedures are being saved, but they become a bit disorientated when they are all being saved in the one network server.

Some of them, for instance, kept wanting to go back to the same computer each time because that's where they had written their program in the first place, but even within one term the change has been tremendous. I'd say that 50% of them are very confident at handling it now. They will ask other children, 'What's your file name by the way?' and read their friend's procedures into their computer to see if there's anything there which might interest them.

We didn't teach them what the implications of the network were immediately. Later on when someone came rushing around from their terminal to someone else's to say, 'How did you do that?' we seized the chance to say, 'Well, you could call it up on your terminal'. Then the idea spread like wildfire.

I have to say that I don't think there is any particular value in being able to call up someone else's work on your machine. It's just as useful to go over to someone else's terminal to have a chat. What is useful is to have more than one machine available at a time because that does stimulate more discussion. If children are working simultaneously on a number of machines on different projects the potential for sharing and swapping is enhanced. They are always interested in what other people are doing and they will frequently go and have a look at what is going on in another group.

I don't know what will happen as other classes begin to work with the network. Children do naturally seem to prefer peeping over each other's shoulders to passing information down a network, but those who have used computers regularly for a number of years may have quite a different attitude by the time they get to this stage.

I love them to share ideas; the value is in discussion, whether or not they are making full use of the machinery.'

# 11 TURTLES AND TOPICS

Brenda Butler is the computer coordinator at Green Close Primary School. At the time of my visits she had a class of nine to eleven year olds, housed in a pleasant old room with wooden floors and large windows running along two walls of the room. The children worked at tables grouped informally around the room and there was a carpeted reading area.

I visited the class in November 1984 and again in February 1985. Mounted on the walls were some sketches of old cartons and tins under the caption *Could some of these empty tins and cartons be recycled?* On the wall of the corridor outside the classroom was a display of still-lifes of fruit in a bowl sketched in pencil. Brenda Butler commented on the children's love for fine detail. She has to work very hard, she says, to overcome their reluctance at this age to work in bolder, looser styles with paint and brushes.

On the morning of my second visit, however, two groups were doing paintings of volcanoes, inspired by a recent television programme. At two other tables children were using batteries, bulbs, wire and buzzers to make simple circuits. Others were busy with mathematics and English.

Green Close has a very active tradition of interest in the arts and drama. Each year the leavers put on a play and while I was there a group of fourth year boys and girls went off to a local dance festival dressed in Indian tunics and trousers or saris, to perform some dances which they had learned from an advisory teacher who comes from India.

Throughout the top of the school children are set for mathematics and English. Work in these sets for two, hour-long periods takes up either one morning or afternoon session each day. During these periods the children move to the classroom of the teacher responsible for their set, returning to their own teacher for the rest of the day.

## The computer equipment in the classroom

As part of the Walsall LOGO Project Brenda Butler's class has the full-time use of two computers. An Apple running Apple LOGO is kept at one end of the room, and a BBC, with Acorn LOGO, the Wordwise word-processing package and a printer, stands at the other end of the room under a window.

The children work in groups of three and Julian Pixton, the Project coordinator, comes in one day a week to help them, as well as Christine Caswell's Project class in the infants.

Print-outs of a number of screen Turtle pictures and related programs were mounted and displayed on the wall: DESIGN, AIRWOLF, STREET, COCKPIT, OWL, NIGHT, FIREFOX and CASTLE.

## Some subprocedures

At this stage the children's programs consisted of a considerable number of subprocedures. FIREFOX, for instance, which was a detailed drawing of a jet aircraft, consisted of:

```
TO MISJLE2
TO MISILE1
TO WINGS1
TO RADAR
TO COCKPIT
TO JETS
TO WINGS
TO TURBO
```

Each of these subprocedures contained a number of instructions — such as BK 150 RT 45 FD 100 LT 90 — which told the screen Turtle where to go and whether to leave a trace or not.

CASTLE drew out a crenellated castle, with a closed drawbridge, three windows and a flag. At the end, several birds flew past.

In NIGHT1 a van appeared, followed by a line across the screen for the road, three stars, the moon, a lamp post then a bus stop.

OWL consisted of a rather angular bird, but with eyes, beak, tail and claws clearly defined.

## A project on explorers

On a display board was some work connected with a project on explorers.

Beside a painting of Christopher Columbus's Santa Maria was a computer drawing of another ship and the following explanation:

● The Good Ship Adele. This ship was made on the Model B BBC computer. We programmed it in because we were finding out about Explorers. Lisa's picture (of the Santa Maria) gave us the idea. The people who designed it were Anthony, Chris and me. We called it Adele because she wanted it named after her.

(This was a reference to someone in the class who was not a member of this particular trio.)

I asked the children whether they preferred working in groups.

'Yes. It's much more interesting in a group because you can talk to other people, and if you go wrong other people can put you right.'

'What about bugs?'

'You always get bugs . . . you always go wrong somewhere . . . but it doesn't matter what you do wrong, you can always put it right again. You can learn off mistakes.

We've copied all the programs out on the word processor, so if the disk was wiped or something you've got a copy of it and you can type it in again.'

One boy said, 'I like the planning. I like being able to make things and invent things: sometimes I get ideas off the telly.

Making the planning come alive is part of the fun. When you write something like **FORWARD 50 RIGHT 90** it looks boring, but when you put it into the computer and it draws it, it comes alive.'

I asked whether he would enjoy typing in programs which had been invented by other people. He said, 'No. I feel proud of it as something I've made because it's mine, nobody else's.'

Several of the girls had drawn lorries or cars and the mixed groups seemed to work well. There was a strong sense of the programs belonging to everyone who had helped to make them, illustrated at one point when, as I was saying into my tape recorder that a program 'belonged' to Jamie, he immediately added '. . . and Chris and Anthony'.

## Combining LOGO with control technology

At the beginning of January 1985 Julian Pixton introduced to the class the idea of extending work with LOGO to control technology and by the time I saw them in February a number of projects had been completed.

Junction boxes are small, white plastic devices, roughly 30 centimetres long. They can be attached to the computer by a lead at one end and a variety of devices — such as buzzes, switches or lights — can be wired up to plugs which fit into holes in the side of the boxes. The boxes used in Walsall have six ports numbered from one to six. After wiring up a light to outlet 1, for example, the children could write a procedure in LOGO which would cause the light to flash on and off in a planned sequence.

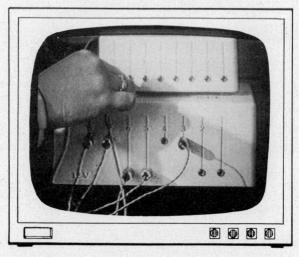

*A junction box allows devices like buzzers, switches or lights to be attached to the computer and controlled by LOGO.*

### A waterfall

Three girls had used this facility to make a model of an illuminated waterfall which they had seen during the annual September illuminated show at Walsall's Arboretum.

Their explanation, with diagrams, was displayed on the wall behind the model.

● THE CONSTRUCTION OF THE WATERFALL:

First we got two pieces of wood and joined them together. We got a
piece of cardboard measuring 90 centimetres. We folded it into four
steps then we made some sides for it. Next we covered the steps with
silver paper to make the lights reflect. The lights needed to be
wired up and we wired them up in threes. Then holes were pushed
through the cardboard so the light would show. Then we put dark
blue paper on top of the silver.

Here was our first problem. The lights didn't show through the dark
blue cellophane. So we changed it to light blue cellophane. On top
of that we put green cellophane which was cut into strips. Then we
stuck them on. We hoped that the green and blue would make the water
look real. Using the lights the water should look like it was
moving. To make it look real we used papier mache rocks which we
painted grey with hints of green.

(At that point the lights were connected to the computer through the
junction box and a program written to coordinate the sequence.)

```
To WATERFALL:

TUNE REPEAT 20
FALL 1 REPEAT 20
FALL 2                and
END
```

FALL1 included the following commands:

```
SWITCH ON 1
WAIT 2
SWITCH OFF 1
SWITCH ON 2
WAIT 2
SWITCH OFF 2          and so on.
```

I asked how they had decided on the sound, which was an effective
watery cascading noise.

'The sound came out of the computer. We just messed about till it
sounded right. At first it all went wrong because we had forgotten what
the correct commands were to get sounds, but Paul, who had made a
level crossing with the control boxes, helped us.'

Although they couldn't explain why it was such fun they thought that WATERFALL was certainly the best thing they had done so far. 'We didn't think computers could do that. We had thought they were just for playing games.' They will be using it in the end-of-term leavers' play.

One of them had written a poem to go with the model:

● The fresh flowing waterfall trembles and tumbles down the jagged rocks, splashing as it goes. The dark weeds grow in the crystal clear water. It flows into the silver stream and down into the hill. The searching watering tail looks carefully in the squelching mud and under the dangerous mossy rocks hiding snails the velvety moss cushions the drops falling from the waterfall.

## A pelican crossing

The group who had made the model pelican crossing, two boys and a girl, explained to me how they had done it:

'Well first of all our teacher who knows all about the technology things (Julian Pixton) was talking to us about traffic lights and he asked us to discuss in our groups what we thought we'd like to do. We were talking about traffic lights and then we thought that a pelican crossing would be more of a task (challenge), much harder.

We made a rough picture as a plan, then we went to see the crossing. We thought there would have to be the two sets of lights, a pavement, a road and the crossing, with studs on the road. We knew we would need three bulbs each for the traffic lights at the front, then two each side for the red and green men.

We started off by painting some cardboard tubes for the poles of the traffic lights, but we found that that was too flimsy so I made one in balsa wood. That was a bit lopsided and while I was away somebody made one from balsa wood.

We cut out two shapes the same, glued them together with a sort of Polyfilla we made out of sawdust and glue mixed together and used it to cover in the gaps. The hoods over the lights were made out of washing-up liquid bottle tops.

When we got to the pelican crossing we realised that the buzzer sounded for a much shorter time than we had expected. And we had got the sequencing of the lights wrong. We had thought it started on the red light, but we found out that it started on the green. So we had to change ours.

We used the computer for the programming. The wires leading from the two green lights came down to the same point on the junction box and were wired to one input. They were plugged into the box at the point numbered 1. We did the same for the red and amber sets of lights.

We decided that since you wouldn't see the buzzer any way we would have it completely off the board so it was positioned off the model and plugged into its own outlet.

We did an overall program called TO TRAFFIC. Then we put in:

```
PAUSE
BUZZER
GREEN LIGHT ON
CROSSING
GREEN LIGHT OFF
RED MAN ON
RED MAN OFF
FLASH AMBER LIGHT          and
GREEN MAN.
```

In fact the title was bigger than the actual program!'

The whole project had been written up and was displayed near the computer. It included photographs taken by one of the group showing the excursion to check the sequencing of the lights and described the actual times involved in detail.

The display included a list of the procedures which they used to program the lights and buzzer and a description of the snags they had encountered entitled *Pelican problems*. These seemed to be connected mostly with the construction and wiring. There was no mention of bugs in their procedures.

## An alarm system for a museum

A third group, which also included a girl, had incorporated pressure pads and buzzes into an alarm system for their model museum. The idea had come from a light sensor they had seen in a local shop. The junction boxes were used to connect the computer to the buzzers and pad.

Adele wrote the following account of their project:

●   We started by using pressure pads and experimenting with noise. Then we had the idea of the alarm. Matthew thought of having the alarm in a museum with a chest containing coins on show so we got two planks of wood together.

    We then decided to have lights flashing on and off while the alarm was sounding. We put the light up to the top right hand corner and we put a pressure pad on the base and covered it with carpet, made a chest and put some old coins inside. I decided to put the chest on a cushion so I made one.

The LOGO program for museum included procedures called TO BEEP, and TO ALARM.

# The class teacher discusses her LOGO work

Brenda Butler explained how she had become involved with LOGO and how her class had reached this stage:

'Though I have had a post of responsibility for computers for several years, my main task originally was to manage the machines we had, making sure that they were taken from the store and put into the correct classrooms every day, and organising programs which might be useful to the school.

At that point we had a number of Tandys which had come to us from another computer project, which were mainly used for skills-and-drills programs that had been developed at our local teachers' centre.

Programs like that have only a limited usefulness so when the opportunity came to use computers in a more creative way this interested me particularly.

I went to a course about Big Trak LOGO run by Julian Pixton. At that stage I knew nothing about LOGO. The first thing we did was to invite Linda Spear, the other coordinator, to visit the school with a Big Trak to show the rest of the staff. It was at the end of the summer term and during that time I persuaded my godson to sell me his Big Trak, which I took into my class and began to use with a group of my seven and eight year olds.

I introduced it as an extra-curricular activity which they could have fun with at lunchtimes, because I wanted to see how they would react. Gradually, over a six week period, I introduced it in class time, till it became part of our general class activities.

The parents began to see its value and, realising that we needed several in a school of this size, with more than 300 children, they gradually bought us some more through the PTA.

During the following term Linda Spear came in regularly with a BBC and a floor Turtle, and shortly afterwards the school bought a BBC of its own.

Linda came in one day a week to work with the older children, starting off with the floor Turtle, and she also used the Big Trak with groups of children. Initially, because we had no means of moving the computer around easily, she would take twelve children at a time to work with her in a resources room. They would do their planning with her and use the computer as and when they needed it. The groups came from several classes so that we could spread the experience as widely through the school as possible and when she worked with Big Trak she was able to go into the classrooms and work alongside the teachers.

Part of Linda's time was spent with me personally. In our school people with scale posts are allowed an hour a week to develop their area of the curriculum in whatever way they decide is appropriate, while someone else covers the class. I spent half-a-term, six or eight sessions, with Linda teaching me one-to-one, introducing me to the screen Turtle and showing me various procedures. As I was a complete novice that inservice session was very helpful indeed.

Then Julian devised a LOGO chip for use with the BBC machine and I used that with my class of seven and eight year olds. The whole school was involved in a road safety project at the time so we used that as our springboard.

First of all we used the floor Turtle in direct drive to design vehicles. After that we worked on the idea of procedures — drawing the vehicle on paper, breaking it up into parts then testing it on the screen before drawing it out on the floor Turtle.

We also used Big Trak and constructed a road with a zebra crossing for it to move along.

I always taught the children in groups. With Big Trak I started with six but soon found that that was too many. With the floor and screen Turtles I have found that four is about right, though I would consider as small a group as three. I may have occasionally used a class lesson when we discussed abbreviations for words like **FORWARD**, to save them time.

*A group of children work together to find a solution.*

As far as class organisation is concerned, I personally like to work with groups, but most of the school works on a class basis. We set for maths and language as you know, and during the setting period children who are not mine have time on the computer which does have the advantage of giving me access to a wide range of ages and abilities.

While groups of children are working on the computer, the rest of the class follows the normal curriculum. We try to integrate the LOGO work into the normal day as far as possible.

Last year there were four parallel classes in lower school and as I took the lower ability range in set time that helped widen the range too.

The beauty of LOGO is that children can work at their own level, right from the beginning, starting with Big Trak. You might get a more complicated or ambitious idea perhaps from the brighter children. But the less able children work just as fruitfully at their own level. I noticed too that they all proved to be capable of great concentration, even children who normally have trouble settling to any one thing for long.

At first they tended to draw angular things like buses or cars. When they had come up against the problem of circles for wheels we experimented quite a lot by walking forward a little bit, turning a little bit and so on, till eventually they got the idea of repeat.

In the beginning, they made monstrous guesses about the amount of repeats they would need and kept going round and round! I had to help them out a little bit at that stage. I think that you have to be prepared to step in sometimes after they have had a chance to experiment if they are getting nowhere. They very quickly realised that the forward distance is the one that alters the size of the wheel, but the angle and number of repeats can stay constant. That was quite a breakthrough.

The following year, I moved into upper school which gave me a chance to work with the older children, a class of nine to eleven year olds. They were a very mixed bunch as far as LOGO was concerned. Some had had experience with Big Trak, some with the floor Turtle and some had had almost no experience at all.

I started them off with a screen Turtle, letting them experiment with forward distances, and get used to distances on the screen, angles and so on, and fairly quickly they got to the point where they could create scenes with more than one item in them.

I gave each group roughly the same amount of time though if they were using the time well I might allow three-quarters of an hour or even an hour. In that time they get their planning done, try things out, learn to edit — there is a great deal to be done. Some children complete a project fairly quickly, others can take several weeks.

I find that they work well now in groups. They enjoy the planning aspect of the work and have become more aware of its value. Working like this with LOGO has made them more sympathetic to each other and more willing to listen to someone else's point of view. I think they have come to value each other's opinions more. They may not always agree but they will listen.

I have only come across one child who was indifferent to working with LOGO. She just sat back and watched the others for quite a long time and seemed quite uninvolved in all the chat and plannning that was going on in her group. She didn't even have the confidence to load the disks herself. The others didn't urge her to help, they just got on with their own project and for two or three sessions we couldn't draw her into it. But even she has since become interested.

At first I used to think that the excitement came from the novelty value, but I don't think so any more. So many of the children have computers at home now that there must be something intrinsic in what they do here that keeps them interested. I think it is a challenge to them. They have become so quick on the keys that if things aren't turning out quite as they want them to be, they can edit very quickly. They think very quickly and they look on the work as a sort of puzzle.

They don't give up. If one day there isn't time to finish, they save the program on disk, load up the next time and carry on. Their programs have become so complicated that they can spend a considerable amount of time on each one.'

*Did you notice any difference in the work girls and boys produced?*

'At first the boys all seemed to produce vehicles like rockets or cars and the girls tended to go for houses, trees, patterns and scenes, and the boys were more interested in variables. But the mixed groups work very well and they have all taken to the control technology with enthusiasm. That really has been a great success.

Though ideas for the models have all come from the children, they haven't sprung as directly out of our projects as some of the earlier screen Turtle graphics did. In fact it has worked the other way round this time. When the children who were working with the control technology got busy wiring up bulbs and buzzers it all looked so exciting that the rest of my class have begun to explore magnetism and electricity. So now they too will learn those skills.

We've recently been given a word-processing chip for the computer and have bought a printer so the children can copy a bit of creative writing into the computer.

They have used it to compose and print out the ad-lib bits for their swan song leavers' play, for instance, which has been a lot quicker than having it typed out and run off in the usual way.'

*Where did she feel she should go next?*

'I feel very much now that I'd like to consolidate the work we have done, not only in my class but throughout the school and disemminate it further. I want to make sure that no children have missed out on the experience. I'd like to do a bit more inservice work with teachers here so they can have time to come to terms with LOGO and develop the confidence to have a go with it for themselves.'

# 12 GIRLS IN CONTROL

Janice Staines' class at Delves Junior School is also part of the Walsall LOGO Project. In January 1984 she began using LOGO with a third year class. Half of that class moved up with her into the fourth year and the present class consisted of 25 ten and eleven year olds. The children who had not been with her in the third year had worked with Big Trak, but had had no Turtle graphics experience before September 1985. The class is almost equally divided between boys and girls.

The children usually work in pairs and on average each group has half-an-hour per day on the computer plus another half-an-hour planning session.

The class has access to two computers every day except Thursdays when Julian Pixton, the Project coordinator, brings in two more. Most of the machines are BBCs equipped with Acornsoft LOGO or Logotron, but there are also two Ataris with Sprites.

Janice Staines runs an integrated day with her children. During my visit a group was using felt and cotton to make finger puppets. Another group was transferring on to canvas, outlines they had planned on squared paper, to be filled in with wools.

Suspended from the ceiling were white cardboard mobiles of birds, connected with a recent project on flying. On display nearby was some writing on the theme *I wish I could fly* and collages of shop windows.

Janice moved from group to group while Julian Pixton concentrated on the children working at the computers, acting as a consultant and trouble-shooter.

## The children's programs

The children showed me some of their favourite programs.

### Tilly the turtle

TILLY THE TURTLE is a program which a boy and a girl had been working on for several months on and off. The idea came from a story they had written on the computer using Wordwise. They then decided to break it down into chapters with a Turtle graphics illustration for each chapter.

The shapes of Tilly and her friend Henry were drawn out using two of the Atari's four Sprites.

The story starts off with a 'phone call from the Mayor asking Tilly Turtle to investigate the theft of the Eiffel Tower'.

In scene two Tilly and Henry drive to the chip shop for a meeting with the Mayor. What they learn there leads them to Heathrow airport for a flight to Paris. The screen graphic shows them in a car zooming off to the airport.

Scene three shows the arrival at the airport. The children programmed the Turtle to draw out the airport's electronic gates then erase them, to simulate the gates opening. The car drives in and the gates close behind them.

Next they walk into the airport's entrance and its sliding doors open and close.

The pair had just started scene five which takes place inside a hangar at the aerodrome.

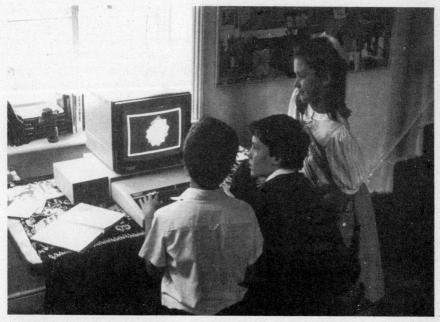

*Children working hard with some Sprites.*

## A spacecraft

Two boys showed me SHUTTLE, which despite being the first program they had made, proved to be ambitious and complex. It shows a spacecraft with a chequered nose-cone and a chequered door which was made using an Acornsoft LOGO primitive, or command, called **STAMP**. This allows them to change the shape of the Turtle as they wish. Having worked out one chequer shape they were able to repeat it across the screen to make the chequered pattern.

The shuttle also has wings and jets with flames coming out of them and a USA sign up one side. Each section of the drawing had been planned out in detail beforehand and there were seven or eight different subprocedures altogether.

## Some Christmas stars

Two girls designing complicated Christmas stars printed out copies for me to take home. Another pair was beginning to draw a snowman and a third was editing a Christmas scene. This drew out a table laden with food and people sitting round it. The words **THE ROBINSON FAMILY IS GETTING READY FOR ITS XMAS DINNER** appeared at the bottom of the scene. It had taken twelve periods on the computer to get this far, they told me.

Several children had made elaborate abstract patterns of the kind I had seen at Ickleford. I was struck by the speed with which girls and boys who had apparently been using the computer for only a few weeks could change and edit their procedures. It was like watching an expert knitter or lace maker at work.

## A treasure map

Two boys were using coordinates to draw out a treasure map. Janice Staines explained:

'I had been talking about coordinates with the children and this pair wanted to use the idea for their treasure map. One of the LOGO primitives allows the children to use coordinates to set the screen Turtle's positions. They can set first one coordinate then the next and the Turtle automatically moves, leaving a line between them. So instead of trying to get the Turtle to turn through exactly the correct number of degrees each time to draw the outline of the island and the grid, this enabled them to get it drawn out far more quickly.'

## A burglar

A girl who was moving the next day allowed me — after some hesitation — to see BURGLAR. It was night and a house was drawn out with a street lamp beside it. A man went in through the door of the house. A dog appeared outside. As the man reappeared the dog bit him. The man ran off and the dog, after a brief leg-lifting stop at the lamp post, followed suit.

# Using the music facility of LOGO

Music is one of the LOGO facilities that this class has begun to use. Janice Staines, who has written a paper about it, explained to me how this had developed. She was presented with a specially written Turtle graphics package for the BBC machine which included a *toot* command. This would accept inputs for volume, frequency and duration of sound.

At first the class experimented with it and began incorporating toots into their programs at various stages, to signal that the Turtle had finished a particular task, for instance, or merely to make the loudest, longest toot they could manage.

Eventually they discovered how to write a procedure to produce a simple tune by typing in several toot commands one after another. Later they found out how this could be extended by using REPEAT.

When the class was given their Atari machines the manual revealed that its LOGO had two toot facilities and that the music note A had a frequency of 440. After trudging round a number of music shops, Janice discovered a list of the frequencies for other notes and the children were then able to teach the machine to produce tunes. By the time of my visit the inputs had been simplified so that when the name of a note was typed in, the machine would emit the correct sound.

Two boys had made an animated Christmas sequence and wanted the tune *We wish you a merry Christmas* to play while the graphics unwound. As I watched they put in the notes, then programmed in the duration and volume for each note in separate, parallel sequences of instructions. When the tune was played back, it was slightly wrong, because they hadn't put in all the correct durations for crochets or quavers, so they had to go back over their procedures to find and correct the bugs.

## A Christmas carol

Another pair of boys explained the origins of their program called SILENT N, which they had been working on for the past four weeks, four times a week.

'Just before Christmas we were thinking about doing Christmas cards. We decided to draw a picture of a cottage with four windows, a chimney and a TV aerial and snowflakes falling around the house. We defined the Turtle shape to make different snowflake shapes and stamped them on the screen. To show that people were asleep inside the house we put ZZZZZZ in different sizes coming out of the window. While the scene is drawn out the tune of *Silent night* is played.'

## Stars in the Christmas sky

STARS consists of a sky full of different-sized stars with the words *Santa flies South* as a heading. The tune *Every star shall sing a carol* had been copied from a carol book. Santa was supposed to appear in the sky, but when they showed me the program a large Turtle flew across instead. They went back into the **EDIT** mode to check the program and discovered that though they had made the shape of Santa they had forgotten to tell the Turtle to collect it. As they discussed how to correct this bug Janice came over to have a look and give advice.

The children explained how they had used a variable procedure to make 13 stars of different sizes. The second part of this program called SCENE showed the interior of a house. One of Santa's elves comes down the chimney and puts the presents out.

# LOGO and control work

Like the top junior Project class at Green Close this class had recently been introduced to control technology using switch and control boxes. Several projects were underway.

## A house and garage

Displayed on tables near the computers was a *microgarage*. It was a model of a house with a garage attached, made out of cardboard boxes. The door of the garage was attached to a motor linked to the computer through the switch box which could pull the door open or shut. On a road leading up to the garage two model figures sat on a model motor bike. In front of them was a vehicle made out of LEGO bricks with a model figure sitting in it. The boys attached a magnetic sensor to the car which had been wired and plugged into a port of the control input box. Concealed under a manhole cover in the road was another magnet also attached to the computer.

The procedure they had written activated the motor controlling the garage door once the car had passed over the manhole cover. The door slid open, staying open long enough to allow the car to be pushed into the garage, after which the motor reversed direction and was pulled shut.

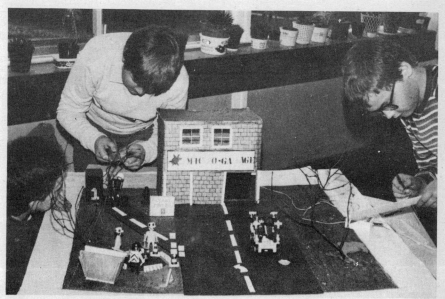

*Building 'Microgarage'.*

## A road scene

A second model, mounted on pegboard, was balanced between two chairs standing on two table tops pushed together. It was a newly-painted road scene. A pub with outdoor seats and umbrellas stood on one side of the road on green-painted sawdust. On the other side were four little model houses and shops with lights inside. Lining the street was a row of street lamps fitted with small bulbs. The girls who had made it explained that their list of procedures included **STREET, LAMPS, HOUSES, ON, OFF, SWITCH ON, SWITCH OFF, TURN ON, TURN OFF**. They ran the program and the various sets of lights went on and off in sequence. I left them wrestling with a soldering iron under Janice Staines' supervision in an attempt to wire up the lights for the pub.

## The Houses of Parliament and Big Ben

A group of boys was working on a large-scale model of the Houses of Parliament and Big Ben. They had built a clockwork control of cogs which moved the hands of their model clock. This was linked up to the computer. The finished program would cause the hands to go round. A magnetic sensor, when activated, caused the computer to chime and the hours to strike. They had written a program which arranged for the hours to strike in sequence. Once the sequence reached twelve it began again.

The whole enterprise, construction and programming, had been carefully planned out in a computer project book. The group said that the procedures had not been difficult to work out though they had needed help from Miss Staines in the beginning. In fact, they seemed more concerned with matching the sizes of the balsa wood fencing to go round the model than with the program for controlling the clock.

## A street crossing

A group of girls had made a model street crossing with traffic lights at the junction and a bus stop, a post box, a telephone box and a bench at the corners. They had observed the sequence of lights at the crossing near the Houses of Parliament during the class visit and, having wired up the lights and plugged them in to the input boxes, had written a program to reproduce the sequence. The program had taken them about 15 minutes to create.

# Refining procedures

Julian Pixton was going over a print-out of the Big Ben program with the group who had made it. They were trying to tidy up and clarify the procedures and make them easier for other people to understand. He pointed out that **SWITCHON 7 WAIT 1**, for instance, could be made into a little procedure on its own and called **MOVE HANDS**. If procedures were refined and labelled in this way, he said, it was easier to isolate and correct a bug when it occurred.

He explained another useful aspect of LOGO: 'Because LOGO stores procedures as text and not as numbers it is possible to load procedure files from a disk into a word processor, make a space between the various procedures and put in some explanatory text. While they are at it, the children can swap the procedures around if they want to put them into a different order. When that disk is loaded back into another computer it will run the program in the amended order. Just as a word doesn't lose its meaning when it is moved from one part of a sentence to another, so the programs still make sense even if the order they are run in is changed.'

## A discussion with the class teacher

*I asked Janice Staines about her background and how she had encouraged the developments I had seen in her class.*

'I was maths trained and started off intending to be a secondary school maths teacher. But I am also interested in history, science, English, art and drama and realised fairly early on that I would be happier in primary education.

When the school received two Tandy computers I set about learning how to program in BASIC. Then I decided to try out a bit of the BASIC with my children. After two terms they had just about managed to put something on the screen, which wasn't very satisfactory. Shortly afterwards I went on a BASIC summer school course, and that's where I saw Big Trak for the first time. That looked like something which I could use more effectively in the classroom, so I came back and nagged the head to try and get me one. In the meantime I went out and bought one myself, and started using it with some eleven year olds.'

## Her early work

'At first I would set problems for the children to solve, an approach I wouldn't use now. I would say, 'How would you draw a square using Big Trak?' and they would put in a progam using seven or eight procedures. Then, to introduce the idea of repeat, I would challenge them to do the same thing in say three procedures.

We used it for science experiments as well as shapes, such as testing its performance on different surfaces and slopes. Then in the summer of 1983 I attended a Big Trak and LOGO course organised by Julian Pixton and Linda Spear. That showed me the possibilities of letting children use Big Trak for projects they themselves had chosen, rather than on work directed by me. It was also my first encounter with the screen Turtle.

I started work on LOGO with just one BBC machine fitted with Julian's Turtle graphics chip. Before going on secondment to coordinate the Walsall Project he came into school and did a little inservice here with us. Then I showed small groups of children how to switch on the computer and set it up and how to go forward, backward, right and left.

When the LOGO work began the other children were so interested that they would rush from their seats and go to the computer when exciting things happened. It took me a while to cope with that, but since I work an integrated day anyway there were no serious organisational difficulties involved in getting going.'

## Her present work with LOGO

*How does the LOGO work fit into your classroom routine during a typical week?*

'The children are organised into groups, each of which may be doing different things at the same time. We have to fit in a certain amount of maths and language work each day. Usually I have three groups going at any one time, one of which will probably be a computer group, one for maths and one doing language work. We also have a session for science or topic work each day. In addition we have three or four periods which are used for art and craft, etc, and PE and swimming have to be fitted in. But it's just a matter of organising the timetable and the children into manageable units and then moving from group to group as I'm needed, including the computer groups. Our day has become slightly more hectic, but it's worth it.'

At the time of my first visit many of the children were designing programs with Christmas as the theme, but they were producing very different end results. The second time, the range was even more impressive. There seemed to be no pattern to what they were doing.

*How is it, that the children are doing such varied things with their time at the computer? How had that variety developed?*

'I have never started everybody off on a specific project. I ask them what program they want to work on and the ideas come from them.'

*Did she decide on the pairings?*

'Usually the children decide themselves who they will team up with and they are very sensible about swapping around if it doesn't work.

On average each child in my class gets half-an-hour a day on the computer. At the moment, because we are doing the control technology some of them are getting much more, but that's just a one-off thing. Because we are short on control boxes (we've only got one for the class unless Julian is in), half the children are having to work on science projects involving control through batteries rather than the switches, etc.

They are trying to think up projects that they can transfer when it's their turn to use the computer control technology. Some have designed a set of disco lights made up of a circle of card with different-coloured sections which revolves in front of a bulb. After half-term they will be able to use the motors to control it and have music playing at the same time.'

*How important is planning?*

'I don't actually insist that they plan beforehand, but I encourage it because we haven't got enough machines for them to sit at and play and still get things done in the short time they each have at the computer.

If we had say 30 machines in the room I would be happy for a child to go straight onto the machine if he or she was happy working that way and could get results by just typing commands straight in. It's the way I prefer to work myself. But for most of them planning is the most important part. They can't cope without it. They need to break things down into manageable parts, then they can go to the computer and try them out.

I started out allowing them to have free rein, and comparing their early results with their later work which they had planned, was instructive. Some children would just sit and type in programs, which sometimes worked. But if they had a bug it was difficult to pinpoint because there was no organisation they could follow. They would have to go back through the whole program laboriously.

When that happened I was able to suggest that they break programs down a bit more simply, so the planning began to develop fairly naturally. Even so there are children working now, particularly with the Atari, who can just sit and type in procedures without any problems, so it has to be kept flexible.'

# The benefits of LOGO work

*In what ways had her children benefited from working with LOGO?*

'When these children came to me they were very fractious, with no idea of how to work in groups at all. They had come from a very formal classroom and they couldn't share ideas, let alone pencils, crayons or anything like that. They were badly in need of certain social skills, to be able to talk to each other and to appreciate other people's ideas. They had to learn how to plan together and then to put those plans into operation.

By the end of the first term of working with LOGO there was a noticeable difference in their maturity. They had been the sort of class which made you think: 'Crumbs I can hardly wait till July to pass them on to someone else.' It's difficult to believe they are the same children now.

In the past it was usually true that if two children were supposedly working on the same thing, one would be doing the work and the other sitting back doing nothing. But I have learned that at least when they are working on LOGO both are learning equally and that they are working cooperatively.

In the language area I find that the amount and quality of their spoken language has improved. They're more keen to discuss what they are doing with me and with their peers. Like many primary school children they used to find it hard to confine themselves to the subject during a group discussion for instance, but that is no longer true.

I have always encouraged chatter in my classroom, but it is still surprising to come upon a pair at the computer talking away and to find that the conversation isn't about say, something they did last night, as one might expect. It is always about their program and what they are doing with it. They can go on like that for anything up to an hour, totally engrossed in what they are doing, which is remarkable for such young children.

The strategies they pick up through using LOGO flow over into other subjects as well. When they go on to long multiplication, for instance, they apply the same strategies for thinking to problems involving multiplication. They identify what the problem is asking them to do, break it down into manageable parts, then put them all together to make the total. And the same applies to problem solving in science.'

*Has the LOGO work cut down on the amount that children produce in other areas of the curriculum? Is there any subject she is unable to cover at present because of it?*

'The only real gap I have at present is with drama. We tend not to do much except for an assembly or if it is part of the project work, but that is the only thing I can think of.

I've had a certain amount of hassle over the relatively small amount of work that appears in the children's subject area books. For instance, you might not find any specific maths covered in my books for say five days or so, but equivalent work has been going on, on the screen. As it is kept on disk we could produce records if they were needed. People sometimes need convincing that important learning can be taking place which isn't recorded in a book. Fortunately, the parents have been quickest to realise this. I had expected some pressure from them but they never questioned the fact that we're using computers or why. They've just been knocked out by the work that they've seen.'

*Had she noticed any differences between the children in her class who had just started working with the screen Turtle and those who had started the previous year?*

'When my original group started they preferred to draw simple shapes like squares or houses which were just triangles and squares fitted together. But though the group starting now have also begun with squares, triangles and rectangles, they put them together in a much more complex manner.

I think that's because this second group has been able to see from the work of the more advanced children what LOGO is capable of achieving. They see at once how you can achieve a very complex picture just by using simple procedures. The boys who made the SHUTTLE are a good example.

It's not just that they see what the others are doing. The more experienced children assist them, which is something I encourage. The children in the present technology group know that I'm expecting them to help the next group when their own projects are finished. I don't see myself as the only person who can teach them. They can learn from each other too.

*Experience can help in solving problems.*

The more advanced children haven't been completely weaned off Turtle graphics. They are still working with the Sprites on the Atari, though the programs they are making are still pretty complex, controlling four Turtles together.

The pair making TILLY THE TURTLE have been working on that on and off since the summer. They do other things in between.'

## Introducing the music work

*How did she introduce new features like the music? Was it left to trial and error?*

'One healthy thing about children is that if you introduce them to something that they are not ready for they will just ignore it. I hesitated about teaching them about variables because there didn't seem to be a natural lead in. But suddenly this year some groups wanted to produce different-sized stars or presents. They were using a different procedure for each item and that was a golden opportunity to say, 'Look you can produce different-sized rectangles with just one procedure'.

I introduced the music originally to my group of advanced programmers, showing them what the procedure did and how to put their own programs into it. When they found a tune they wanted to use they would come to me with the music and we would use a comparative chart to work out what the names of the notes were, since most of them don't read music. Then they put those into the computer. Now they can help each other when the need arises.

We've also been able to control things like synthesisers and drum kits through the computer. Using LOGO you can put them all in sequence to make quite a snappy little tune. That is an important facility because though the children were quite happy to put in tunes they'd found elsewhere, they weren't so willing to experiment with music of their own. This is one good way of getting round that reluctance and we shall be developing it further. At the moment we are also working on rounds and canons and setting different voices for the computer to use.'

*Might it not be better, to encourage children to experiment at a music table with real instruments?*

'Possibly. But this enables children without musical ability, who can't read music, (a) to learn to read music indirectly by a sort of matching process and (b) to integrate music into their cartoons, which is a facility no other piece of equipment can give them. I'm not suggesting that this sort of work should replace music making of the traditional kind. So far the sound is pretty horrible, but as techniques improve the children will be able to orchestrate, for instance, at an early age.'

## The stages of LOGO work

*If she were beginning afresh now, with a class which had never used LOGO, how would she proceed? What stages would she expect to see them go through?*

'I think I'd still start with Big Trak because the children see it as a toy and it is fun for them to handle. It introduces all the basic LOGO primitives for Turtle graphics like **FORWARD** and **BACKWARD**, turning **RIGHT** a certain amount, and **LEFT**, but through a device they can actually handle.

Once they fully understood forward and backward, and could estimate distances, I'd move on to rotation. Next I'd get them to choose their own projects, perhaps designing a game for someone else to play or making say a space station for Big Traks to move around.

At that stage I'd introduce a floor Turtle. Once again, it's a tangible object that they can see and handle, but linked to the computer. I'd let them use it in free drive at first so that they can see exactly what it is capable of doing. Then they could work on a project of their own choosing, like a house.

Next I would introduce the idea of simple procedures by teaching the Turtle to draw the square part of the house then a triangle for the roof, and put the two together.

I'd probably go on to things like **REPEAT**: 'How many times do you have to repeat **FD** and number and **RIGHT** and number to make a square, etc? How do we have to vary that to make a pentagon?' while looking at relationships between the turns they make and the number of sides and so on.

Once they'd got that firmly understood I'd point out that they could do similar things without the floor Turtle, on the screen. I'd use the same sort of system for developing screen Turtle work as I had with the floor Turtle, and leave them to develop from there.'

*What other aspects of work with computers did she want to explore?*

'There are other things, word processing in particular, that we want to develop. We have dipped into data handling, but we want to do more with that. We've got the QUEST program for data retrieval and as industrial archeology will be our project next term it will be useful for that.

We also have the modem in school which means we have access to Prestel and other distant databases. I'm particularly interested in expanding that. We can also link up with other schools through Telecom Gold and our great ambition is to get in touch with MIT (Massachussetts Institute of Technology). When we do the children in my class will be able to talk to children over there, so we can compare what's going on in the two countries.

I also want to expand the music, controlling synthesisers through the midi interface, not just with LOGO.'

(A midi interface enables an existing school microcomputer such as a BBC to be linked to a stand-alone electronic keyboard.)

# 13 HOW FAR CAN YOU GO WITH LOGO WORK?

Marlborough Middle School, Harrow, North London was one of the six schools taking part in the Chiltern LOGO Project, headed first by Richard Noss (now at London University) and now by Katrina Blythe, on secondment from the Headship of Ickleford Primary.

LOGO work started in 1982 with a class of nine to ten year olds and their teacher, Deborah Booth, who was given an Apple computer with LOGO and a Turtle. Carol Berezai was teaching the parallel control class, which had no computer but began to pick up some knowledge through team teaching with Miss Booth. She and other members of staff began to run computer clubs in the lunch hour with groups of children to get some experience.

'I panicked because the children were already into list processing. But I found that it is best to learn with the children. This implies a certain relationship with the children and it is very important to recognise this.

I have found that it is essential to put in lunchtime and evening work to help them find the answers to problems.'

Mrs Berezai's present class of eleven to twelve year olds consists of two groups. One half, part of the Project group, has been using LOGO for three years. The other half, who had been with her in the third year, had had only a few months' experience.

The catchment area of the school is a mixture of working-class and middle-class families. About 30% of the children come from Asian families, most of which are Hindu.

The class is run as an integrated day and during my two visits a number of different activities were in progress.

On the walls the displays included sketches of owls, a set of pictures and writing about *Jealousy*, *Greed* and *Avarice*, which appeared to feature portraits of the children, pictures of winter scenes which were part collage, part paintings, and some work on *The history of wheels*.

There are two computers in the classroom, an Atari and an Apple II. Both machines are popular with the children who use them for different types of programs. The attraction of the Atari is that it has four Sprites as an integral part of the LOGO. (In some versions Sprites are an optional extra, which can be added on with the purchase of special 'Sprite boards'.)

It may be worth reminding readers at this point that a Sprite is a Turtle whose shape can be changed through the use of a grid on which the appropriate outline can be drawn. At Hillary Junior School two girls had used Sprites to draw out their animated garden program.

Each Sprite can be given a different colour, or speed or path from the other three and each can be controlled by an individual set of procedures. This gives children access to an extensive range of variations with which to work as they build programs using Sprites, as I was soon to see.

In this class the children, who work in pairs, have a session on both each week. My visits disrupted the normal proceedings to the extent that groups were allowed to come out in turn to 'show off' their favourite programs to me, but while they did this the rest of the work continued unchecked.

The children did not find it easy to articulate their evident enthusiasm, nor could they always explain precisely what they were doing. The Atari was particularly popular because of the Sprites, colour and sound, plus the fact that they can make 'really good arcade games' on it, though some found the Apple easier to use.

'I also like it when you can make two shapes and when they collide the screen flashes and a whole lot of notes come out of the computer.'

## Some examples of children's work

At playtime one boy was allowed to stay in to design me a special procedure. After 15 minutes he had produced a pattern of beautiful, multicoloured traces which looked like a shower of shooting stars or fireworks.

Two girls had drawn a crenellated castle with windows. They were using two Sprites to draw out a woman's shape, one with a hand down, the other with her hand up. They intended to write a procedure which would flash the two shapes onto the screen alternately so that the woman will seem to be waving from the castle window. The idea came out of their current class project about castles.

I was shown several more programs.

## Changing stars

In the program called STAR a star was drawn out and then wiped, to be redrawn a number of times in a different colour. The background colour changed each time a new star appeared.

In SUPERSTAR a circle of complicated stars was drawn out. The colours of the stars and the background changed a number of times. The colours were gorgeous.

## A violin plays

In VOTRON a violin with strings was drawn which appeared to move as if they were being plucked while the background colours on the screen changed five times. 'It was a bit hard because I wasn't used to it but it's still one of my favourites. BASIC is pretty hard but LOGO is easy. I like doing stunts like racing cars going round a track. That's being made on the Atari but I haven't finished yet.'

## Superman flies

In SUPERMAN a set of six skyscrapers was drawn out in black against a blue backgound. An animated figure of Superman, complete with cape and boots flew overhead while the Superman theme played. Superman was made up of three different Sprites, one for the figure, one for the boots and one for the cloak. At one point they went into the **EDIT** mode to show me how they had set the speed of the Sprites to coincide so the figure appeared to be one shape. In doing this they disrupted the sequence so when the program was run again the Sprites had got out of sequence, causing Superman's various parts to float across the sky in a disintegrated fashion to their intense amusement. (Since the original program was on disk, the damage was only temporary.)

## Batman theme music

With BATMAN there were no visuals, but the Batman theme music was played.

## A football player

In the program PITCH a football pitch was drawn with a man on it who ran about. It was planned to put in a football for him to kick and to add some music.

## Rockets and meteors

Two boys described one of their favourite programs:

'We called this one POW! and it prints random dots all over the screen. In a moment rockets and meteors and things like that will go over the screen. I got one of the shapes wrong.' (This program had music too.)

I asked why a mouse had suddenly appeared in the midst of the rockets and stars.

'That shouldn't be there. We got rid of one of the rockets by accident. What happens is that when two of them meet, there are things in the Atari called *When Demons*, and when two of them meet you can have an explosion.'

They said that each group had a file in the class disk and that POW! had taken about seven hours of class time to create. They sometimes came in at playtimes or lunchtime to finish off projects.

## Hickory Dickory Dock

One current project was an animated version of *Hickory Dickory Dock*, with the music in the background.

'It's not very successful at the moment. The clock face won't draw out correctly and the mouse runs up the clock too jerkily. POW! was a lot more successful.'

## Freddy the Pacman

In FRANTIC FREDDY a very complex maze appeared on a pretty blue background. Building the maze had used up most of the machine's memory so they needed to use a second file to make the procedures which would guide Freddy, a Pacman figure, round the maze. A joystick attachment had been added which was supposed to control the Freddy-shaped Turtle, but at present Freddy tended to go through the walls of the maze and generally to behave erratically. Fixing Freddy was the next job.

Two other boys were working on a maze for their Pacman. The one they had made already was too simple.

## Some very advanced LOGO work

The following conversation conveys something of the flavour of the children's relationship with their teacher and their attitude to working with LOGO on the screen.

Carol Berezai explained the background:

'Two particularly bright boys are working in a way which I think will become more usual as children become more experienced with LOGO and start using it younger. One has had three years' experience. The other, who has only had one term, is very bright and has picked up a lot from his partner.

The story behind what they are going to show you is from a maths investigation we were doing in which we were trying to make an ellipse by folding paper. We had got the idea from Johnny Ball's *Think of a Number* book.

We managed to make a true ellipse by paper folding and I took it further with the maths group those boys are in. Could we find a mathematical definition for the ellipse? We tried making cardboard models, plasticine models, all sorts of things to try and work out whether the angle you cut the cone off at makes different ellipses, and if so, why.

They then set up drawing an ellipse on the computer which looks an awfully boring procedure, but a huge amount of work has gone into it. They tried it various different ways and personally I don't think they are going to manage it because the screen distorts the image. I was also told at a BLUG (British LOGO Users' Group) conference that it's impossible, but they are trying to do it anyway.

They are now on a tack where they have plotted an ellipse on a piece of graph paper and they are going to put in the ellipse by the coordinate method.

That's the sort of use I see LOGO being put to, as a tool for maths, which I think is very important. Not just for maths either, but as a resource for the classroom, that they use when it's needed, like an encyclopedia or a dictionary is used now. They know enough about computers now to be able to decide when they are appropriate and useful or not, and are confident to use it as one resource.'

The boys then tried to explain to me what they were doing. I understood very little of what they were talking about.

'We are trying to draw a perfect ellipse. We use two different commands to do it, one which was my idea and one Mrs Berezai's idea, which was using an extra command built into the computer called **ARC**.

We think we may possibly have got an ellipse, but it doesn't look quite right, which may be the fault of the screen.'

They then ran the program which produced what looked like a convincing ellipse to me, except for a section at the top and bottom which joined the two arcs at the sides together.

'We made it up of two different arcs; the two side arcs are the same and the bits to join them at the top and bottom are a little subprogram to join them up.

It's **ARC RIGHT 90**, which is the radius of the circle if it does the whole circle, and 90 is the amount of degrees it does of the circle. Then it does a much smaller one — **ARC 10** — for the top and the bottom. They are 90° as well, and it does them twice.

It was setting up the scrunch to the normal that was the thing. You have to **SET SCRUNCH** to get the screen to work properly.'

Me (faintly, and lying in my teeth): 'I see.'

'Then you have up **FULL SCREEN**, then it clears the screen, hides the Turtle, **PENUP LEFT 90 FORWARD 20 RIGHT 45**. That gets it in position, then **PENDOWN** and then it starts drawing it out.

This didn't actually take us that long to make, just put a couple of arcs together and it worked quite well. There's another procedure which took a long time to work out, but it didn't really turn out to make that much of an oval at all. This one has been more successful.'

## Testing a mathematical theory

*What, I wondered, did they think was the use of this sort of equipment in the classroom?*

'It's got a lot to do with maths; all the working out of radiuses and lengths, for instance, it helped with that.

Maths helps you to use it and it can help you with maths as well. There was some working out we had to do once, and instead of typing those things out on a calculator we had a go at writing a program on the computer.

We called it Mrs Berezai's Theory. She worked out this thing with two lots of three digit numbers. If you get one three digit number, reverse it and take the lower number away from the higher number then you get 70. You keep on doing it again and again and eventually you get 198.

Or 99. Sometimes you get 99, which when doubled is 198. That's the Berezai Theory.

So we tried it out with two figures, four figures, five figures and so on, but instead of doing it on paper or on a calculator we tried it on here with a program. I think what we did was type in the name of a program with two variables, which were the two numbers you wanted to add, then just adding a variable to another variable and minus-ing it and times-ing it, and things like that, then printing out the answer at the end.'

*Was the theory proved at the end?*

'I don't think it works.'

Other boy: 'It did for three digit numbers. We found out that for two digit . . .'

Carol Berezai (calling across from where she was working with a group): 'It was ever such an exciting project!'

Boys: 'Because she thought it up! We called it *The Tedious Berezai Theory* and made a poster about it, but we didn't call it that on the poster.

We found that sometimes it worked with two digit numbers and sometimes it didn't. We didn't actually get to five because it took us so long to write five digit numbers. We found it was really easy if the numbers were consecutive. It worked really well.'

*Happiness is solving a difficult problem.*

## Assessing the children's progress

I spoke to Carol in class.

'Every now and then I give them a challenge which provides me with two things: some idea of where they have got to as individuals and also a means of bringing the class together round a common theme. The breadth of ability has become so wide now that I like to do that now and then.

The challenge I set them came from a book by Tim O'Shea and John Self called *Learning and Teaching with Computers* (Harvester Press, 1983). It's to draw a little stick figure with a triangle head, to be placed in the centre of the screen, with identical figures on either side, so that there are three on the screen at the end. The point is that it is possible to use repeated subprocedures to build up the final shape. To place the three figures on the screen they have to make an interface which moves the figure from one place to another.

Each pair has two computer goes to do it in and on Friday we will have a look at it to see how everybody got on.

It is a good task to set because the lowest ability children can get it done by direct drive if necessary, so everyone will have something to show at the end. The more advanced immediately saw the possibility of using subprocedures to save time, and that there are several different ways of getting them positioned, some much more sophisticated than others. You can set your position by coordinates, or direct drive it.

It gives me some idea of where they are happy, because sometimes you give them an idea and they reject it because it's too soon, but giving a task like this shows me what immediately comes to their minds and what they are happy doing.

It's a way of assessing the children without threatening them or forcing them to compete. Everyone can produce something which I can praise and it gives me a chance to see where some consolidation is needed. I can go back over areas where they are obviously a bit shaky and give them a bit of a push in that direction.

The two brightest ones were given the additional task of making the first figure bigger and the third one smaller than the central person because I knew they were capable of that. They needed to use a variable and did so quite happily.'

I came upon the pair who had been told to produce the receding set of three figures. They had done it as instructed.

'We were going to put in something flashy, like going through all the colours at the end of the sequence, and we were going to make one of them wave at you, but we haven't had time.'

## The teacher's previous experience

I spoke to Carol at the end of the day.

'I was a typical Cockcroft girl — failed maths O level three times. I started off teaching RE and sociology in secondary school then, because I didn't like teaching secondary school, was lucky enough to be able to transfer to middle school. I then studied for a part-time diploma in maths education and was maths coordinator at my last school. I came here as a Scale 3 with responsibility for maths right across the school, from five to twelve.

When I came to Marlborough, two years ago, the children were working on the floor Turtle with Deborah Booth, who was part of the Chiltern Project. By the time I took on the third year class in parallel to hers they were into screen work. During the year they began things like list processing, which I used to see across classrooms.

I moaned and moaned and eventually was given a floor Turtle, which we started to use in February 1984. When Deborah left I knew that I would be inheriting half of the original Project class so I took the computer home and did a lot of work myself.'

## The children's development

'At the moment half of the class has had less than two terms of experience with the screen Turtle and the other nearly three years of it, but the difference now is in ability, as opposed to LOGO work. A lot of the children have almost caught up on skills because being with the experienced ones, having access to two machines and lots of computer time, has enabled them to learn from the others and to catch up.

Each pair has two hours a week, one on each machine. Some were in groups before they came to me which were based on friendship, not ability, but now the ability range has become very wide. Some children are still working in direct drive on the screen, others are far beyond anything I can manage. So we have had to juggle the groups around to match up abilities rather than sticking to friendship pairs.'

## LOGO is a powerful tool for learning

'One of the beauties of LOGO, particularly with Sprites, is that even the least able children can produce patterns and things which whizz around the screen, so there is an inbuilt success level.

There have been problems. It very much depends on how you want to teach. This is only a personal view, but I think that LOGO can only really work as a tool for what you are trying to do. It hasn't any value in itself, but it is useful for what I'm trying to do which is teach the children independence, problem-solving skills, logical thought and language development.

Those are things that I would be trying to teach with or without LOGO, but LOGO provides a powerful tool that I can't provide myself. The children can set their own level at which to work, so it is completely mixed ability. We keep trying to provide children with relevant problem-solving experiences in school and it is hard to find ways of doing so. But LOGO does offer them such situations.

They set their own tasks and since they need to learn certain skills to solve them, they learn to break the work down into stages which automatically provides them with sets of problems to solve. It's easy to learn by mistakes because the screen can be wiped and they can start again or the procedure can be debugged in a flash. It allows children who aren't particularly able to gain a great deal of confidence because while the working-out stages aren't on pieces of paper for everyone to see, there is an end product everyone can admire. It's got an inbuilt success to it, as well as providing the appropriate amount of challenge for each child, set by that child. These are all the sorts of things I would want to provide for them.'

## Classroom organisation

'As I work an integrated day, with different groups doing different work through the day, it wasn't difficult to find the time to work with computer pairs, especially at first since they just start off using the four basic commands FORWARD, BACKWARD, RIGHT and LEFT. The teacher's role changes according to the group.

There are times when you aren't actually busy teaching other groups, when they are free to come to you for help with a particular thing they want to do, but haven't got the skill or knowlege to get on with alone.

But quite often there isn't time to give them that degree of teaching during class time so you have to fit it in during hymn practice or playtime or lunchtimes. The time element does become a bit unpredictable as they progress.

It's difficult to say whether using LOGO has crowded out other parts of the curriculum. If you run a complicated, integrated day, working with groups, there are always going to be occasions when you feel that someone may have missed out because you were dealing with another group just when they particularly could have done with some help. That's true if they are painting or writing a story, not just working out a LOGO problem.

I think that at the beginning, when I wasn't too sure of myself, there was a tendency for me to spend too much time with the LOGO groups because I was so worried that I might not be doing the right thing. In fact I was worried that I might be interfering too much. It's hard as a teacher to acquire the skill to just grit your teeth and walk away from a situation. It would be so easy to say, 'Oh, do so-and-so', to nudge them, instead of leaving them to get on and do it for themselves. That has receded now, but the problem of not being free to intervene at precisely the time when I am needed is still there, but it goes for everything we do.'

## The children set their own tasks

'I give them an outline and within those very wide parameters they set their own tasks. I may say, for instance, that if they are working with Sprites they must develop a sequence with their animation that holds together. Quite often our topic work will be reflected in the things they come up with, like those girls who were working on the castle.

Sometimes I actively encourage that sort of connection. When we were doing a project on food they were at the stage where they were making the big step of producing circles and a lot of them were frightened to try because it is quite a complex thing to do. I suggested that one week everybody drew a graphics picture involving food, including plates with hamburgers and fried eggs and so on, to encourage the production of circles.'

## The differences between DART and LOGO

'As far as the differences between DART and LOGO are concerned, I haven't actually used DART except with the infants. The two difficulties I can see with it are first that there is not enough space in the memory for all the subprocedures they need. The three figures in that challenge, for instance, probably are made up of four, five, six subprocedures and that's quite a simple task. When they get to more complex projects they use a lot more procedures and DART just doesn't have enough memory to record them all.

The syntax also worries me because it isn't logical. That matters particularly when they go on to list processing when it's important to have the same logic going all the way through. Since you can use LOGO to drive the Turtle as well as more complicated things I think a school would be better off going for a full LOGO if they can afford it, right from the start.'

## Two success stories with LOGO

'There have been two outstanding successes with LOGO in this class. One boy, who is quite big for his age and has had trouble producing tidy, accurate written work, has been very successful with LOGO.

He's taken to list processing which is a difficult concept, and has used it to make up quizzes. The procedure he really enjoys is a joke procedure, which asks questions like, 'What is a cross between an elephant and a blackboard?', that type of thing, with a joke answer. Behind a program like that is a lot of complicated work. It involves a lot of statements like, 'If the answer is A then do B, if it's F print out Y.' You have to be able to think in quite a structured way to make a joke questionnaire because there are a lot of *ifs* to deal with. But he has mastered it.

Now he is in here every lunchtime queuing up to work on the computer. Currently, he is trying to produce a Pacman arcade game. It's giving him the confidence he needs. The main effect has been that he enjoys the praise and wants to come to school now. And though this is the age when people like him could have become stroppy, and though he could easily have become a prime candidate, he hasn't.

The other big success has been the boy who made that instant program for you. He is of limited ability and has to cope with a whole host of domestic difficulties. He has trouble forming relationships with adults and other children, gets into scraps and so on, but he loves the computer. It's his own special little world. He comes in at lunchtime and often works alone, though he is equally happy to work with a partner. Perhaps it's a fantasy world that he can escape into. Some of his programs consist of cars which crash into each other. Maybe that helps work off his aggressions. Last year he was quoted as saying, 'I hate school, but I come because of the computer'. I worry a bit about what will happen to him when he goes to secondary school, though.'

## The teacher shouldn't have all the answers

'I think that LOGO works best for a teacher who has a relationship with her class which allows her to admit that she doesn't have all the answers every time. Even with all the skill in the world they are going to come up with problems that you haven't a clue how to answer, particularly as they become more advanced. Quite frankly at least two of mine are producing work which I can't understand a lot of the time. So I have to be prepared to say, 'Show me how it's done; you teach me how to do it'. You have to be ready to cope with the times when they ask you how to do something and you have to say, 'I don't know the answer. Let's sit down and try it together'. Sometimes it works, sometimes it doesn't.

So far we have managed without outside help by a process of trial and error. After all, it's the process we are after, not the product.'

## Introducing LOGO into a school

'In September I'm leaving to become a maths advisory teacher in Harrow, and part of the job will be to disseminate LOGO throughout the borough. We will be working with schools who want to get involved. It's important that the schools should decide for themselves that here is a need for LOGO, and be prepared to devote a machine to one or two classes full time. That's vital. You can't have it one day a week or half-an-hour here or there.

We have said that as a start there must be two classes in the school with teachers who are prepared to get involved and we will provide them with a LOGO chip, a floor Turtle and a printer to start them off. I think they will be able to learn from our mistakes.

It's important to have support in a school. I was lucky to have a supportive head as well as an expert in the shape of Deborah. It's a big thing to take on in your classroom. We used to spend hours on the phone and at lunchtimes, talking about better approaches to this and that. 'I made a mess of this. How can I do it better?' It's not so much an expert you need as one other person at least to talk to, to share the experience with as you go along.

As this was a research project we probably pushed some of the children along too far too fast. At that stage, since it was research, we had no idea of how far children could go, how much they were really understanding.

I now give them a set task occasionally, like the three men assignment, to find out what needs consolidation. We've also learned how to present abstract things like list processing through working with cardboard models, which show what is going on inside the computer in a concrete way. The children can put various labelled signs into marked boxes so they get to see and manipulate physically the things that are happening in the machine when they build that sort of procedure.

When we teach recursion we actually make out work cards and say, 'What do you think is going to happen?' Then they try out the work card and see what happens and we talk about it in general. It's quite a complicated mathematical concept, calling on a procedure that you have made to go on repeating itself till you tell it to stop, but now they have got on a lot faster on the Atari with recursion to do things like put a random number of stars in a sky.

Looking back, I'd spend more time on things like subprocedures with some children. It's not always true that because they have used a process once or twice they have really understood it.

I would do a lot more work off the screen when we got to the idea of random numbers, as well as on the screen. But I think most teachers would automatically stop and consolidate at each stage in a normal class situation. Being in a research project was different.'

## The benefits of LOGO work

'I think the children are getting from LOGO the benefits I hoped it would give them. They approach new work with confidence now, particularly maths problems. They will always have a go even if they can't always do it. It may not all be to do with LOGO. It may be a general class ambience. I don't know. But I see a lot of questioning, a lot of 'Why? What if? What for?' You can't get away with anything with this lot.

My class tends to get into trouble for being cheeky. Supply teachers can find them hard to handle, but whether it's LOGO I don't know. They've become used to me saying I don't know and quite often they will turn that back at me when I press them.

Orally they are far and away better. They love debates about things like where motorways should be going, in which they role-play. I tend to work like that anyway, but they are now used to questioning, to talking to each other as they work at the computer and in other aspects of their work. They will generally consult each other before they come to me.

So a lot of the benefits are social and emotional and that's difficult to prove, isn't it? I can prove to you that they use it as a resource, that they understand things like *random* which they might not otherwise have done, but a lot of the rest is gut feeling.

I don't personally think that you are likely to get children more advanced in primary school than the two boys you saw today. They are streets ahead of anyone else in our class. The girls making the castle are more like the norm. Certainly if you were going to consolidate as you went along you wouldn't get so far.

In addition, these children have access to two or three machines all the time so they have probably had seven years of normal experience within the three years. Nobody else will be working in that situation.'

# Headteachers talking

*See page 197 for the program to produce these rabbits.*

# 14 THE DEVELOPMENT OF A SCHOOL POLICY

At this point it seemed that the experiences of some of the headteachers who had seen LOGO working in their schools might be useful.

Sandra Penlington was involved in the Chiltern LOGO Project from the start. She has now moved to a school in Buckinghamshire.

'I first saw LOGO working at a course run by MEP for heads in the spring of 1982. They showed us a number of different things we could do with computers and I liked the Turtle work best, so I went back and asked my borough for it.

When Harrow decided to join the Chiltern LOGO Project our adviser remembered my nagging and thought he'd let me in to keep me quiet.

We were given an Apple computer, a colour monitor, a disk drive and a floor Turtle. They were put full time into one classroom with a class of nine year olds and Deborah Booth. They had computer time every week and so we started to learn about LOGO.

Richard Noss, the coordinator, would come in and work with the children several times during the week. He asked us not to give it to the parallel class, so that they could act as control and I agreed, on condition that they be given a set of equipment after the control period ended in February 1984. At about that time we got our BBC micro which we gave to the first school staff. They decided to run DART with the floor Turtle we bought from school funds.

At this stage all of the first school, middle and top infants were having some time with the floor Turtle and in September of 1984 we got another computer which the second year of the middle school was able to have.

The third year had use of the computers at lunchtimes and after school in computer clubs and I was angling for another machine for the first years at the time I left. I actually think that there should be one machine available to every year in a school.

In the infants, the computer coordinator worked out a timetable so that they each could have it one day a week, on the same day each week. It would be taken from the store and set up in their class first thing and they would use it all day. They worked in groups of four so each child would manage to get a turn during the day.

There were surprisingly few variations in the way the children progressed, considering the differences in the teachers' backgrounds, and in their teaching styles. Some were probationers, some had been teaching for five years, some were close to retirement. I was lucky in that all of them are good, solid class teachers.

The teachers had informal meetings at which they worked out what they were going to do with the children, which may explain why the work tended to be similar. Deborah Booth helped them plan their strategies and had regular workshops with them. While I took school assembly they would meet in the staffroom and work out what the next stage was going to be.

Luckily, we had a caretaker who was computer-mad. He knew where to plug them in and how to switch them on and off. We were lucky too that we didn't have a lot of equipment breakdowns and that when we did we had the Project coordinator, Richard Noss, to come in and fix things. Deborah and I could also get things going at a pinch, so were probably able to cope with the hardware better than the average school.

We devised a curriculum guideline for LOGO as we went along, throwing out things we had tried which didn't work, keeping effective approaches and trying to put them into some kind of order.'

## Our early difficulties

'Probably the worst thing we did at the beginning was to make the teachers set up the hardware and load up all the disks. It was terribly time consuming for the teacher to have to load in a new disk every time a group changed and it turned out that the children were perfectly capable of doing it themselves.

After wrecking a Turtle more than once we learned that one child in the group had to hold the cord to stop it being stepped on or tugged loose.

We found that a lot of the younger children had great difficulty with turn, because they didn't know their right from their left. We'd been mulling the problem over for weeks without coming up with a solution when one day a class teacher, who was by no means a computer expert, came rushing in and said, 'I've got the answer'. She devised some small cards with arrows on, so simple and easy, but it worked a treat.

Another mistake we made was to put the pen straight in when we started them off with the floor Turtle. As the children had no sense of distance the Turtle would run right off the paper and draw a line on the floor, which irritated the caretaker. To keep on his right side I would have to be scrubbing the lines off. So we learned to wait until they had a good estimate of distance before putting the pen in. Once the pen was in it became a point of honour with the children not to let it draw on the floor. The other thing we learned was to let the children decorate their own Turtles because they are far more creative than we are and they can make it assume whatever character they want it to have that day. If it's going to hospital it can have a plaster on, if it's unhappy the mouth can turn down. It always seems to be a male character, oddly enough.'

## The advantages of full LOGO and Sprites

'We had both DART and a full LOGO. DART is a Turtle graphics package which was written for the BBC machine before full versions of LOGO became available.

I can't see the point of children learning DART when they will eventually want to go on to use full LOGO because there is more in it. For instance, they may want a program which allows you to draw a picture and put a caption underneath. Or where you can move the picture and text around the screen and put them where you want them, so you can have, say, *Happy Birthday* in the middle of a card. They couldn't do these sorts of things with DART.

There is no question that your bright, primary school children benefit from a full LOGO. And I feel now, having used Ataris for only one term, that you have to give them the Sprite facility as well, because they need the movement and the sound, so that they can make animations, which is something they all find very attractive. Their experience will be diminished if they don't have the full set of facilities at their disposal.

Before we got the Ataris they would desperately try to animate by using **PEN ERASE**. They made an animated program for one of the title sequences on the Open University video, but it was very unsatisfactory because it was so slow.'

# From the floor to the screen Turtle

'We prepare them for floor Turtle work with activities like games in PE and movement lessons, then the teacher usually introduces it with some full class sessions. They are shown the basic commands and how to move it around the floor then, if they are very young, they have one or two sessions with set tasks like putting the paper bin in the middle of the floor and seeing if they can guide the Turtle safely round it and so on.

In general the teacher decides when the children are ready to move from the floor to the screen. There comes a point where they are starting to do things like drawing circles, which take ages with a floor Turtle. Once they understand that you make a circle by going forward a bit then turning a bit, and they can write a procedure, then they are ready for the transfer. Ours usually know what a subprocedure is too, but I don't think that that's essential. What they really need are very good concepts of distance and turn. They shouldn't still be making mistakes like forgetting to type in the inputs and they should have done **REPEAT** on the floor.'

# My role as headteacher

'As head my main job was to be barrier between the teachers and the outside world. Deborah Booth in particular was inundated with people wanting to come and visit her classroom and I had to say no on her behalf.

I had to make sure I knew what was going on with LOGO myself, and to keep an eye on what was after all an experiment. I was answerable to the parents as in every other activity within the school.

I would go and sit at the computer with the children two or three times a week, even for short periods. When Deborah went off to Hatfield for inservice work I would take her class and that gave me a chance to work with the children. And if they had done a particularly good project they would come for me to go down and admire it.

But during the first 18 months in particular, when we were punching back the frontiers, I spent about an hour-and-a-half per week with Deborah, discussing what was going on and where the next problem would be. Sometimes it would take up a whole Saturday too. It was a very time-consuming job. She would talk and I would listen.

Several members of staff were afraid of the technology, not LOGO itself, but the machine. They are still afraid, but they use it because the older children set it up for them so they don't have to handle the plugs and the rest of the hardware. They can simply concentrate on teaching strategies which they have thought out with other members of staff.'

## The benefits of LOGO work

'One of the main advantages of LOGO is that it's not like other areas of the curriculum where you have to give them something new frequently. One little bit of information lasts the children for a long time, particularly at the beginning.

It speeds up as you get towards the end. The end? There is no end as the children get older, but because a tiny bit of information from the teacher can last weeks at the start it builds up the teacher's confidence and gives them a breathing space in which they can rush ahead a little bit.

It's important to have somebody on the staff who has done it all before, that they can run to. I think LOGO is unique in many ways because it makes children think for themselves. Where problem solving and logical thinking are concerned I have never found its equal. There are books for maths coming on to the market now I know, attempting the same thing. But they don't have the same impact as LOGO. A LOGO program is made by the child so it's theirs, the books are still the teachers, and you'll never cap that.

I found the children more outgoing, more interested, more keen to come to school. I can't say it was just the LOGO. Perhaps it was the atmosphere that LOGO engendered in the classroom.

It's my personal opinion that it improves teacher quality. Well, it made me a better teacher, because I learned to keep my mouth shut. How many times do we as teachers go over the top with children and continue to push them when in actual fact we should leave them alone? With LOGO, because it was new, I was having to develop fresh strategies to use with the children. I learned to keep quiet occasionally and not to go on too far.

Now the children do that with you. They pick you up like a reference book, and when they've finished with you they put you down again. That's pretty hard for a teacher to take, I think. So I think it improves quality of learning and of teaching. I can't think of any better reasons for putting LOGO in your school.

*What about trying this key?*

One child had had very little success in school — he was clumsy and slow, but you see him at the keyboard and he's an absolute wiz. He has simply found that he can do something. Now I know that often happens with computers because they haven't tackled it before, but where LOGO is concerned there is actually no failure for the children.

When a child writes a LOGO program, because they know what they want it to do, they will persevere with it until the end product satisfies them. I honestly have never seen a child give up writing a program because they couldn't do it. They do not look on a mistake as being wrong or a failure. They call it a bug and it's simply something that they have to think about and put right.

It helps children with emotional problems, it helps slow learners because they can proceed at their own pace, it helps the bright children who often actually under-achieve because this is something which allows them to go off at their own rate and at their own tangent.

I think amongst the children at Marlborough it's some of the bright ones who have benefited most, because the potential is never ending. Of course even the bright children have to be watched. You can be just as lazy with LOGO as you can with arithmetic. Teachers have to learn when to step back and also to sense when the child is coasting comfortably, just reiterating things she learned some time before. Then they have to be set a challenge.

I don't know where it will take them eventually. We shall have to wait till they have left school.'

## Some advice about equipment

'You can do LOGO with just one computer. We did it with the DART in the infants. But you can't do data handling, word processing and all the other programs as well as LOGO with just the one machine. The only way you can use LOGO in a school is to dedicate a machine to it full time. If I only had one computer, that's what I would do with it. I think it's the best use for a computer in primary schools at the moment. But I would prefer not to have to make that choice because there are other things which are valuable.

We didn't really have to push anything out of our timetable to make room for LOGO. We worked in groups anyway, for language development and maths, so we made room by using those times. LOGO is full of maths and language so that was where we made the space. It helped that the school works on a fairly free and flexible timetable.

I doubt that LOGO could work in a very formal school. To use it effectively the computer has to be on all day so you can have groups going to it all the time, especially if it's shared between several classes. If you work to a timetable which all have to follow simultaneously then somebody will be missing some work all through the day. It won't work. You have to have the work grouped.

Obviously things like PE and music were the exception and during those class lessons the computer was turned off.'

## The demands on the teacher

'It has to be said that it does require a great deal from the teacher. To start with they have to get used to having this thing going on in the corner of the classroom and it's not easy to cope with. It tends to raise the noise level in the classroom. All the teachers involved found that. We talked about it and decided that it was a constructive noise, and we would accept so much and then quieten it.

We have found with Carol's present fourth year that they question what they are given and I can see that this could cause problems if they went to another school or into a class where the teacher did not work in the same way.

I do worry about what will happen to children who are exposed to LOGO at the primary level when they move into secondary education. I think that they may have some quite serious problems in accepting a more authoritarian approach. What is more they won't keep quiet about it. When they are given three pages of arithmetic to do they will ask why when they've got calculators. They will say that because that's the way they've been brought up for the last three years.

It can be very tiring on teachers, coping with such children. Now it may be that I have noticed it because the two teachers who have been running LOGO classes at Marlborough have had the children who are further ahead than any other children. For them every day they come into the classroom has been like stepping off a cliff.

It may be as we become more familiar with LOGO that feeling will go, but both of them have had days where they have been exhausted by the end because a child has come up against a problem and they haven't been able to solve it. Part of my job in that case has been to dispense the tea and sympathy. It can make teachers feel inadequate and there is more that's likely to drag you down when you have to face that day after day.

We've got to do something about the equipment to make sure it's 100% reliable. It's infuriating when things break down and suddenly a group can't do what it's supposed to do. The children get annoyed and fractious and so does the teacher. Irritating on the school management side as well, so we've got to sort that out.'

## The need for a delicate touch

'I'm concerned that people may think that LOGO is the answer to all their problems and it isn't. It can be badly handled and then it won't do what it's supposed to. If a teacher starts sitting at the computer and teaching, it won't work. The children have to be left to take the initiative and they also have to be allowed enough time to work in. You have to be prepared to allow them to run over.

It's very time consuming for staff. Often playtime, lunchtime, after school are taken up, or I will get a message saying, 'Can I keep a group out of assembly?' as they try to sort out a problem.

It's also not all that easy to keep tabs on the child's development. Unless teachers make themselves skilled in assessing LOGO they could get into a state where the work doesn't progress sufficiently and people end up being lazy with it. That's demanding and it requires a great deal of skill.

It's not like handling those other types of programs in the MEP *Micro Primer Pack*. Those depend on a traditional type of teaching skill. LOGO is completely different. It requires a delicate touch. You must be around and have your ear to what is going on at the computer so you can intervene when you are needed. Children will come to you, but sometimes they leave it too long and you need to be aware of when that is happening.

LOGO is child-centred so, though they can work on their own for a lot of the time, paradoxically they need their teacher far more than with their other computer work.'

## LOGO — The best thing to hit primary schools?

'I'll say one other thing. I think LOGO is at a crossroads right now. It has just become available for the BBC, so for the first time LOGO is available for the great mass of primary schools in this country. It will either be handled badly with people taking the LOGO manual and working their way right through it, in which case it will flop completely and people will say, 'I don't see what's in this'.

Or it will be the best thing to hit our primary schools since well, I don't know, perhaps the best thing that's ever hit our primary schools. I honestly feel that if we get the inservice work right, the literature that goes out about it right, then we'll be okay, but it's got to start proving itself.

Marlborough was lucky. We had everything — Richard Noss, going out on inservice training, the works. But we were also very much on our own on a lot of occasions and we had to sort out the teaching strategy to go with it, but I hope we've learnt from that.

Now we've got to put LOGO into schools where something like that has never even been dreamt of. We have to get it going throughout whole schools and see if it will work without any backup. Come spring 1985, LOGO is going to have its biggest challenge when the BBC versions become widely available. If it survives that it will survive anything.'

# 15 DEVELOPING LOGO

I talked to Sandra Penlington's successor, Chris Evans, about his experiences before Marlborough and about his plans for the next stage.

'I was head of Brookside Primary School in Hillingdon for eight years. We were among the first batch of schools to have a computer under the DTI scheme, but though the hardware available was very good the software was pretty appalling, both for the Spectrum ZX81 and even for the BBC, which we got later. It's ironical that now that the software has improved computers like the BBC seem to be very much on the way out as far as many people involved with computers are concerned.

LOGO only became available for the Spectrum during my last term at Brookside and though we had the BBC DART, it didn't have the same capabilities as a full LOGO. It was only when I saw LOGO on the Spectrum that I began to realise the implications for what we could do in the classroom.

I think we were a bit overwhelmed by all the software available and though we were using DART on the screen we may well have been doing the wrong things with it, but there was very little advice around as to how it could be used. There was some training available from the borough, but basically we had to train ourselves. We started at the same time as Marlborough but, as we were left on our own like most schools, our handling of DART was not very successful.

Children drew pictures and we set them little challenges, but I don't suppose we got very far off the ground. We had started to get into procedures and to build up data which you could use. After we got DART I began reading a bit and had begun to get quite excited about what LOGO could do, but I was still very much at the play stage with the Spectrum LOGO.'

## LOGO is far more advanced here

'When I came here it was immediately apparent that they were leagues ahead of us in what they were achieving with the children. I saw young children using technical equipment like a floor Turtle which we had never dreamed of using. At the top end, the twelve year olds were writing programs which I could not comprehend at all. I couldn't understand how they went about doing it.

It was also interesting to see that they were using totally different hardware to the machines I had been used to — Ataris and Apples. They were using a BBC with DART, but it was the way they were working which was so different. They obviously knew what they were about because they had a progressive scheme worked out — floor Turtle with no pen, then with a pen, then eventually on to the screen. These things had never occurred to me.

There was something striking about the learning situation. I went into the infant class one day where they were working in fours. Now normally when a stranger comes into a class of that age the children tend to crowd around and ask questions. They want to know who you are, where you're from, things like that. But nobody from that group was at all interested in me. They were totally involved in their work. It was fascinating to stand there and listen to four young children absolutely absorbed and cooperating, working in a way that was clearly very meaningful to them.

The same thing would happen further up the school with the computer club. I'd see two girls working together and I found that the hardest thing to do was to shut up. You know how as a teacher you like to hear the sound of your own voice. In this situation the important thing was to be quiet and let them try to resolve their difficulties.'

## Losing the fear of making mistakes

'What has become apparent to me in this school is that LOGO is about making mistakes and doing it in a non-threatening situation. Children can make mistakes and they then want to solve them. That is the most enlightening thing about it that I have seen. You never get things right the first time. You always have to resolve problems, mistakes that you have made. I think that often in primary school mistakes can be looked upon as something negative and children spend most of their time trying to avoid them. A computer is not at all threatening. It's not like correcting something which a teacher has marked wrong. Perhaps we're to blame as teachers for getting into situations where the wrong things worry us — and, therefore, the children — more than the right things. It's true that if you are drawing you can start again with a fresh piece of paper but sometimes teachers don't like that because it's wasteful.

Since I've been here I've become convinced of the value of LOGO simply because it is problem solving in its truest sense. It encourages the sort of activity which we as teachers want or try to get our children involved with all the time. With LOGO you can't avoid it.'

## Our equipment needs

'The Project children will be leaving us at the end of the summer term and there are hardware implications involved in the ending of the Project. This school is probably two years in front of most others in the borough and I have been asked what hardware we would need to keep up the level of the work to the present standard.

I think we need a minimum of one machine per year group and that they would have to be committed exclusively to LOGO. It is so big that it is hard to do anything else with the same machine. It takes time. So we would need another floating machine to use for other things people want to try like simulation work, data collection and so on.'

## Encouraging others to use LOGO

'The present thinking is that this will become a feeder school for others in the area to draw on. That may force us to go for machines which are compatible with the ones in most schools. A lot depends on how good the different LOGOs are too, and of course the relative cheapness of a computer like the Atari makes it very attractive, especially as it has such features as Sprites, which the children are mad about.

One of the things we want to develop is inservice work. It's not really good enough to expect people to take a machine home and learn LOGO on their own. There will have to be support, some of which we can provide ourselves from within the staff, but some of it will have to come from the authority, especially for teachers to whom this is totally new.

Ideally, I would like to have one teacher in every year group who is familiar with LOGO and who could act as a resource for the class next door and with others who are less confident and who could coordinate the work across the year group. We will be sitting down to discuss how we can get a combined mixture of inservice work continuing which involves some time for teachers to work alongside each other, perhaps freed from their class by me, mixed with some lunchtime and after school training.

As far as the children go I would resist the idea of a sort of *Five to fifteen guide to LOGO*. It's too flexible a resource and there are too many directions that children can go off in. I suppose you could generalise by saying that all children should probably start off with a floor Turtle, but as far as Turtle geometry goes once they start designing their own problems their work naturally evolves from what they are doing.

It does make tremendous demands on a teacher because sometimes they go beyond her and she can't always be sure how to help them when they go wrong. And a teacher can't expect to say, 'Oh you can't do that'. It is a programming language and they are learning to program whether they realise it or not. So it's very hard to measure a problem they want to set themselves against a problem you want to set them. But it does mean that they will be very independent in their learning.'

## 16 DART DOES WELL

Though many teachers share Sandra Penlington's and Chris Evans's preference for a full LOGO, others see advantages in using systems such as DART and ARROW which offer many of the graphics facilities of a full LOGO, including the ability to drive a floor Turtle.

Ingrid Brindle is head of a Tameside Primary School which uses DART. While she recognised the undoubted value of a full LOGO, she argues that DART should not be dismissed too readily: its limitations may not be so important when other factors are considered. These include ease of access, cost, various practical considerations and, most importantly, the school's curriculum: while a full LOGO may offer a host of subtle refinements, DART may adequately meet the school's curriculum requirements.

'In our school, we are very committed to a problem-solving approach in all areas — science, history, craft and design, music, drama. Our central concern is to encourage skills and strategies for problem solving and DART is one useful vehicle for the techniques we want to develop. While a full LOGO would obviously be welcome, it is certainly not essential for our problem-solving curriculum.

Working with the floor Turtle or using the screen for Turtle graphics work, has the special bonus of allowing the child to develop strategies for problem solving which can be used in all kinds of situations within and outside of the curriculum. In this regard the usefulness of LOGO as opposed to DART is not an all-or-nothing matter as DART is clearly able to provide many of these opportunities. LOGO, however, allows children to explore more complex problem-solving situations within the realm of Turtle graphics and to develop those techniques in other areas such as control and music.'

### Some outstanding DART work

'Some of the work which the children produce with DART is remarkable. Quite a few of our eight year olds have become very comfortable with handling the concept of variables in a practical way to solve problems, which is quite a feat for a young child.

One boy, for example, wrote some procedures in DART which were very elegant. Using only two lines of instructions he was able to draw a window with four square sections, each with a tiny square in one corner.

He then modified this procedure so that a set of tiny squares clustered around the cross at the centre of the window. In one sense, the 'product' on the screen was simple, but an impressive amount of thinking had gone on before the child could produce those graphics images. He then went on to experiment producing a *tunnel* by using a procedure for a square of variable size to grow a series of increasingly large squares centred on one corner; this boy is by no means exceptional.

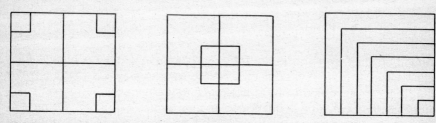

*Using variables to create different forms of 'windows'.*

Some people argue that the mathematical potential of DART is limited. While there may be some things it cannot do, it still offers challenges which are not trivial. I have been running inservice training courses for groups of secondary and primary teachers which involve them in experimenting with DART. Even the maths specialists among them found that they were exploring problems which stretched them.

Children have no trouble adapting to full LOGO when available if they have started with DART and I think there are a number of advantages to starting with it. For one thing, a lot of teachers find it simpler to begin with because it is so straightforward. They are not afraid to have a go at using DART, whereas some of them felt intimidated by the apparent complexity of a full LOGO.

Some enthusiasts may be interested in LOGO for its own sake but most teachers are primarily interested in helping children to learn and are interested in computers only in so far as they contribute to that. The very simplicity of DART is an encouragement to such teachers.

There are also the practical problems to consider. No school in our authority yet has a full version of LOGO. These cost around £60 and that's a lot for a school to pay out, especially when the staff don't know much about LOGO. For the cost of a disk, a school can get a copy of DART from the local resources centre which has an LEA distribution licence.

Then there is the question of computer time. Most primary schools have one machine between an average of around 200 children say. Now working with Turtle graphics is very time consuming and sessions of an hour or so may be necessary to get the most out of it. Now let's say the children work in pairs and a class in a seven form school has the computer once every seven days. That means that each pair of children is likely to get a go only once every six or seven weeks at best. With so little access to the machine, the sophistication of full LOGO with all the bells and whistles may not be quite so relevant in practice as it seems, to the purists, to be in principle.

Remember that, certainly in my school, we want to use the computer for lots of other activities (in addition to Turtle graphics) which we think will contribute to a problem-solving approach to learning, such as word processing, information handling, adventure games and so on. At the moment we tend to deal with the practical problems of using the computer in these various ways by concentrating on one sort of application each term, relating it to our topic work.

Certainly, I've found DART to be very good in persuading teachers to rediscover discovery learning and to rethink their educational philosophy and priorities. People who cannot afford a full LOGO should by no means despair. DART can give children a lot of the essential value of LOGO and can provide one of many microworlds in which problem-solving skills can grow.'

# 17 WHY USE LOGO?

Katrina Blythe, head of Ickleford Primary School, has recently been seconded to coordinate the Chiltern LOGO Project. I asked her to describe her involvement with LOGO in the classroom and what she had learned about integrating it into the curriculum of a school.

'The Chiltern LOGO Project was set up two years ago in the autumn of 1982.

Five teachers were selected from varied types of schools in the region. Some were in London boroughs and mine, in contrast, was a village school.

At that time I was deputy head, with a mixed third and fourth year class. We were given an Apple computer with disk drive and printer, and a floor Turtle. I knew nothing about computers at all when we started. We concentrated on LOGO because we were asked to and it needed quite a lot of courage to get started.'

## Our early experiences

'As a group of pioneering guinea-pigs we had to be coaxed along, but eventually, after being assured that we had picked up enough to get going, we made a start with our classes. We received no training initially. We were simply given a manual which we had to come to grips with for ourselves which meant spending quite a lot of time working on our own at home over weekends and so on. Once we got started we met twice a term and Richard Noss visited us regularly in our classrooms to give us a hand.

Those group meetings were very important. We used them to talk about things like classroom organisation and management — when to stand back and when to intervene, for instance. We learned together as teachers, bringing along our individual ideas to the group sessions, and we changed tremendously over the year.

In the beginning, some felt very strongly that they must stick to Papert's ideas of complete freedom for the children. Others, tending perhaps to the other end of the spectrum, preferred to use work cards and wanted activities to be thoroughly structured. But by the end of the year we all seemed to have come together into a sort of middle position. Sometimes the children had to be given complete freedom and sometimes they benefited from having some instruction which gave them more power for subsequent explorations. In practice we all ended up oscillating between the two techniques.

During the course of the year I got all the children started on the floor Turtle and by the end of the year the range of activities was enormous. Some children were writing numerical or factual quizzes related to their topic or practical work, others were doing quite exciting things with graphics. All had moved off the floor Turtle because they were beginning to want things to happen faster, but some were still at a very early stage, rotating shapes and beginning to work with variables.

It was soon clear that LOGO was a very worthwhile activity. I could see children being fully extended at every level of ability. It was offering something in the classroom to every individual learner and an activity with that sort of scope was certainly worth having.'

## LOGO can increase children's confidence

'I could also quote a number of cases where children's confidence had been increased. One case, which has been written up in the Chiltern Report *Turtleland* (MEP, 1983), concerns a child who cried every day when it was time to do maths. The tears would just lie in her eyes. You couldn't ask her a question in front of the others because that would upset her too much.

When the Turtle arrived her mother asked me not to put her on it because she would find it too distressing, and on the first day she stood behind the Turtle crying, but I persevered. A few weeks later she was in a group and it was her turn to be at the keyboard. I think they were trying to work out how to make a curve and a boy not known for his tact called out, 'You've done that wrong!'

My heart sank. But she just turned around, gave him a huge grin, corrected her mistake, and we had no more tears for the rest of the year. Her maths work was not transformed, but she started to relax because here was a medium for handling numbers and solving problems which didn't frighten her any more.

One of the other attractive features of LOGO was that it enabled children to share their maths. For instance, there was a group of children doing very elaborate procedures to draw a Turtle and they needed spirals for the shell. At that time I encouraged the children to display print-outs of their work around the room so that other people could use them, just as researchers would. This group picked up a spiral which a little girl of quite limited ability had written. She hadn't used recursion, but had worked out another method of increasing the sides as the spiral went round. They asked if she would allow them to use her procedure as one of their subprocedures and of course she was very pleased.

I found that it developed mental arithmetic too. So LOGO was providing a number of the elements which I was particularly concerned with as a maths teacher: arithmetic, exploration, problem solving, investigations, and cooperative learning.'

## Organising the groups

*How did she decide on the optimum number of children who should work on one terminal at a time?*

'After a trial period we settled on a group of three for floor Turtle work. One was needed to work from the plan and decide how it should be drawn out. A second typed in the commands and the third had to keep an eye on the Turtle's movements and relay that information to the others.

When they moved on to the screen we wanted to make sure that there would still be discussion and that everyone in the group remained fully involved in what was being done. Three proved to be too many so we settled on two.

In our determination to remain democratic at the beginnning of the Project we tried to arrange for a spread of ability within each group, and we devoted a lot of time to working out our group splits. In fact we found that if you have an enormous range within the group the quicker child dominates and the slower one starts to withdraw. We learned too that the most effective groups consisted of people of comparable abilities who were also friendly and willing to talk to one other. There was no point in putting together people who were enemies, even if their intelligence levels were similar.'

*LOGO helps children to focus more on processes of learning.*

*What about the length of time the children needed at the computer each day? How long could they work enthusiastically?*

'That varied enormously. Initially we thought it would be possible to have strict half-hour periods which we could tick off on a register, but that didn't work. I came to the view that people should be limited to about 40 minutes, but it seemed wrong to tell a child to stop who had been having a pretty rough time without any success. I would step in and give a hand, allow them another five or ten minutes once they had ironed out the bug, then offer them a new challenge to explore in the following session, so they left looking forward to it.

Equally, if a group was able to complete the project they had prepared within 20 to 25 minutes, and was happy to go away and think about something else, it seemed silly not to make that time available to another pair. That struck me as the most sensible sort of approach and in a class with a flexible timetable and the full-time use of a computer it was possible to work that way, provided one kept track of roughly how long each group was getting over all.'

## A whole school approach to LOGO

*How did LOGO get started at Ickleford?*

'In the second year of the Project I moved to Ickleford School as the head and the Project moved with me. I was given the task of seeing if a whole school could get involved with LOGO.

I didn't, of course, expect the LOGO work to develop with the same speed and intensity over a whole school as it had within one special Project class, where you had a teacher working with a Project coordinator. Obviously this scheme would have to work at a different pace than the original experiment. In any case, I felt that it was important that if a school was going to make changes that they should take place at a rate which all the teachers felt happy with.

As it happened, even with those issues in mind, the way LOGO was introduced wasn't the typical one. Normally in a school you would want to discuss the new aspects of your language programme, or whatever the area is that you are thinking of changing or adding to the curriculum.

But in this case, when I arrived at the school the staff knew that I was part of the Chiltern LOGO Project and would be hoping to get LOGO going, so it was a bit artificial in that sense.

The staff at the school were well established. The deputy had been there for 25 years, and three of the other teachers had been on the staff for 12 or 13 years. We had the advantage too that the school was well integrated with the village and its expectations.

There was already an RML 480Z computer in the school, but it was not being used very much. Several of the staff had been on the introductory computer courses, but they couldn't see the way forward with several small packages and seven classes to one computer, so it was just lying there.

One of the first things I did was to talk to the staff about the Project and explain what it was about and something of the philosophy behind LOGO. I showed them samples of children's work and then I started two teachers off with the Apple system, which was the one that I was most familiar with myself.

I felt that it was important to involve my deputy from the beginning and as another member of staff had expressed an interest in the original computer in the school, although she was a history and art specialist, she became the other pioneer.

As it happened they were teaching second and third year juniors at the time. It seemed sensible to put the effort into children who would be able to develop later within the school rather than concentrating on a class which would be leaving soon.

As I had no class of my own I was able to give them some support and help at the outset. But despite my help they had to do most of the work themselves, as I'm sure they'd tell you, mainly by taking the computer home to teach themselves there. When they felt confident and ready to start they introduced the floor Turtle. They shared the system, using it on alternate days and that was quite nice because they were able to compare notes about how things were going in their respective class-rooms, and it was very interesting to see them going through things we had gone through earlier: 'Should we have told them that or should we have left them a bit longer to discover it?' and so on.'

## Involving the parents

'They worked together during the first term and then I thought it was important to get the parents involved, so we had a parents' evening. We showed them LOGO work and explained the thinking behind it.

One of the things we had noticed was that as the work in the two first classes developed, some parents — naturally enough — would try to help their children by telling them how to draw certain shapes, for instance. Of course by doing that they would be negating the very process we were trying to create. So it was important to explain that it was the process which was crucial, not the end product. It was important that the parents should appreciate what LOGO was about. Once they knew it had been established in two classes and saw the work which was being produced they could relate it to their own children.'

## Spreading LOGO through the school

'Towards the end of the first term I did put a machine of my own, a Commodore, into the top junior class because it seemed very sad that the top juniors could see the younger ones having something which they were denied. Commodore LOGO was very similar to Apple LOGO so their teacher was able to refer to the other two for support, but I wasn't able to provide her with a floor Turtle.

It was another term before I started the next two teachers off and again I thought I'd stick to a pair because mutual support was crucial. This time it was the top infants and first year juniors who shared the 480Z machine with a floor Turtle and a printer.

One interesting point was that though RML has a different LOGO to the others it made no difference to the children. The teachers were able to get support in the early stages, not only from me and each other, but also from the members of staff who had started ahead of them.

We continued that way for the first year, using three machines — the top junior class on its own with the Commodore, the second and third year juniors sharing the Apple system, and top infants and first year juniors using the RML.

The sharing of a machine proved to be quite a good idea. Not having the machine all the time gave them some breathing space, but interestingly, no one in the school would choose to share a machine now.

At about this time the Project decided that it would be interesting to see what would happen if the children had the use of a network of machines. Would they find it more stimulating and would even more cooperative learning take place?

We had a spare room in which a network could be housed and we began to use it in September 1984. We decided initially to make it available only to the third and fourth year classes and that freed another computer for the remaining pair of classes so everyone at last had their own computer.'

## Advice for starting LOGO work

*I asked Katrina what advice, if any she could give to a head or a school which wanted to make a start.*

'A lot depends, of course, on the size of the school and its organisation. What works in one school may not work in another. But a general point that would have to be made, I think, is that LOGO cannot be diluted. You can't have four classes sharing a computer and getting their hands on LOGO occasionally. The children have to have regular access because their problems do become terribly important to them. They do want to get back to the machine so that they can carry on their work and solve the problems they have set up for themselves. If you are restricted to one computer, as many schools still are, then you may find it almost impossible to be fair to either all the children or all the staff.

Ideally each class needs its own computer, although it is possible for two classes to share a system effectively.

LOGO also needs time if it is to flourish throughout a school — time for both children and teachers. However daunting these two factors may appear, the effort involved is amply rewarded by the benefits it offers to the children's learning.'

# Comments and conclusions

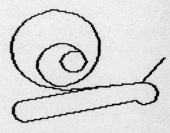

See page 198 for the program to produce this snail.

# 18 THE EVOLUTION OF LOGO INTO EDUCATION

In the preceding case studies I have described pioneering work with LOGO in some British classrooms. Though some of those classes had the advantage of unusual amounts of outside help and hardware and so may have produced work which is untypical, several points of general interest emerged from their activities. The Cockcroft Report on Mathematics called attention to a need for primary schools to foster the development of general strategies for problem solving and investigations. It recommended that children be given opportunities for becoming familiar with such processes as:

— making a graphical or diagrammatic representation, and observing pattern in the results

— making a conjecture and discovering whether or why the conjecture is correct or not

— learning how to solve a problem by looking at a simpler related problem

— developing persistence in exploring a problem

— setting up an experiment and recording the possibilites arising from it.

Cockcroft also stressed the importance of an ability to work with others and to communicate progress.

This is a formidable catalogue and, somewhat dishearteningly, the Report went on to say that little is known as yet about how these processes develop nor are suitable materials for teachers readily available. It commented, too, that 'more study is needed of children's spontaneous problem-solving activities and of the extent to which strategies and processes for problem solving can be taught' and reminded us that skills such as 'classifying, counting, measuring, calculating, estimating, recording in tabular or graphic form, making hypotheses or generalising' which may be acquired in the course of learning mathematics, are also useful for science.

Many of the teachers I visited were aware of Cockcroft's priorities and stressed LOGO's value as a powerful tool with which children could acquire many of the skills referred to in the Report.

They were also familiar with Seymour Papert's ideals and aims as set out in *Mindstorms*; in particular his belief that Turtle geometry could provide a 'tap-root' into creative mathematics.

Many had read of his hope that LOGO might eventually help to bridge the gap between the 'technical-scientific and humanistic cultures' and so to encourage societies to adapt to the creative possibilities inherent in a computer-rich society.

At first reading, these notions though exciting, seemed worlds away from primary classrooms as I knew them. Yet after watching infants twisting their bodies to left and right as they work out which command to type in for the floor Turtle, then ordering it to **RIGHT 90**, I began to see what Papert was driving at, and to get some glimpse of how mathematics and movement can be fused into one aspect of learning.

Many of the teachers in the studies used movement lessons to introduce their children to LOGO. Some took turns acting as the Turtle, moving across a room in obedience to the children's verbal commands, sometimes with hilarious results. Through activities like these, as well as subsequent programming, it becomes clear that LOGO can form a bridge between abstract mathematical concepts and young children's natural inclination to relate new ideas to their own experiences, physical as well as mental.

Older children, such as the classes at Marlborough Middle School and at Ickleford, exploited LOGO as a tool, to do the donkey-work in complicated mathematical investigations, such as the rectangle generating puzzle or when trying to draw a perfect ellipse.

Many of the teachers I visited saw the benefits of LOGO as much more general. They valued it as a problem-solving device, not merely in the areas of mathematics and science, but right across the curriculum. As Papert had hoped, their classes used LOGO to create animations, stories and jokes, to develop complex patterns, or to explore a number of variations on simple shapes such as polygons or semicircles.

I saw groups of children absorbed in the beauty of the graphics they were creating, quite uninterested, for the time being at least, in the mathematics which had generated the patterns in the first place.

Programs such as the space ships or waterfall at Green Close School, or the integration of chimes and music into working models built at Delves relate to another of Papert's notions, which is that children derive particular satisfaction from work which they can see as connected with activities or devices in the adult world.

# The value of microworlds

Towards the end of my travels, I went to call on Derek Radburn, headteacher of Long Clawson Primary School in Leicestershire, who is currently chairman of the British LOGO Users' Group. Though he too is convinced of the value of LOGO for creative programming, he also sees advantages in the access it gives children to microworlds. These ready-made systems use LOGO to generate programs with particular, deliberately defined and limited features.

He explained how they worked:

'You can create programs which show, by means of graphics, how objects move in space, where they are not limited by gravity. So, for example, the child can play around with an object which starts moving across the screen in one direction and doesn't stop until a force is applied to it from another direction. Through this sort of play the child can begin to understand what is involved in Newtonian physics.

Another program might allow you to simulate the movements of limbs in a set of animals living in a particular environment. The child can experiment with the environment and see how the animals adapt to changes they make, in a way which would not be possible in reality. So, if for instance, they make all the food, such as snails, retreat to the bottom of holes, they can see why a creature like an elephant with a long nose might survive, and what might happen to animals which didn't have such convenient characteristics.

One can also write a program which draws out graphics of mountains and rock formations. The child programs in variations on the structure and hardness of the rocks and then subjects each variation to different climatic conditions. By observing the different rates of weathering which occur within each set of climates the child can begin to understand some of the forces at work in the environment, which are, of course, imperceptible to them in real time and space.

As children work with programs like these, as well as devising their own, they gradually develop strategies which they can apply in any situation where they are presented with new information or unfamiliar problems.

There is a LOGO for the BBC, for example, which allows children to explore mazes. This may sound trivial, but using the computer to construct and explore mazes of different levels of complexity, some in three dimensions, is an excellent way of developing strategies and memory and is very good fun.'

Some people, he says, dismiss LOGO as merely a Turtle graphics package, fine for young children to play with, but with no importance beyond that stage. He points out that Turtle graphics can be applied to work on the theory of relativity and the curve in linear space. In addition, because LOGO has the power to be extended into areas like these microworlds, it can provide children with what Papert called 'objects to think with', so they can become more skillful in grasping the processes which make up the world they live in.

*Beverly Anderson on the MEP video 'Turning Point' (see page 189 for details).*

## LOGO and the learning process

Too much of our educational system, Radburn believes, is still preoccupied with the product, what he calls the 'I'm finished Sir, what shall I do now?' approach. LOGO helps children to focus more on processes of learning than on end results. In particular, he says, it allows children who are not naturally good at abstract thought to deal with ideas through having something concrete to 'lock on to'. If they get stuck in the three-dimensional maze, for example, they can order up a version on the screen which is a cross-section or plan, so they can check where they have been and decide where to go to next.

Although I was till sceptical about some of the claims being made for LOGO, I found this argument particularly attractive. Like many teachers of young children I have long been aware that their reasoning powers often exceed the ability to explain what they think and why, just as children can tell a good story long before they become fluent on paper. If LOGO can help to make this sort of facility plain and to develop it further, then it is indeed a valuable tool.

Derek Radburn cited another beneficial effect of working with LOGO: 'Girls in particular — if I may say this without being sexist — tend to look for approval at every stage and need to be encouraged to stand on their own feet. LOGO encourages them to take charge of their learning, to set their own goals and derive private satisfaction from their successes.'

For many of the other teachers too, training in thinking and the development of general problem-solving skills was one of LOGO's chief attractions. They gave examples of children who had become markedly better at planning, organising and constructing models, for instance, in a systematic way. Some were noticeably keener to edit stories than previous classes of a similar age had been. Other teachers detected a shift towards more complex drawing and painting.

Teachers commented too on the extent to which the freedom to invent and solve problems of their own devising encouraged children to be imaginative and adventurous, and even more crucially, to regard mistakes as, at worst, diagnostic. Sometimes a bug would be seized on creatively, and used to develop a graphic, animation or story in a different way from the one originally planned.

In some instances, as the children took control of their learning, their independence showed itself in unexpected ways. A number of teachers remarked on the fact that though children would listen politely to instructions about how to use LOGO in more advanced ways, they would revert to using it at the level at which they felt comfortable until they themselves saw a need for incorporating the new bit of information or technique.

The teachers on the whole were pleased with these developments, regarding them as evidence of just how thoroughly the children felt in command of their learning, and seldom felt the need to force the pace through their teaching. Now and then a few children would be noticed who were happily coasting too long on one plateau of success and these would be encouraged to move on to fresh challenges. One or two teachers had found it useful to issue the occasional compulsory class challenge as a way of diagnosing which children needed to consolidate particular aspects of the programming.

Despite my determined scepticism, the variety of work produced within the schools and classrooms I visited was impressive. Though many of the teachers used informal, group-based methods, LOGO also seemed to fit into more formally organised classrooms. I was struck too, with the sight of classes such as the six year olds at Marlborough, working unsupervised in an orderly and systematic fashion, as they guided their floor Turtle round a complex underground roadway.

Without exception the teachers I met praised the development of the children's social skills which they felt LOGO encouraged. Many saw such training as its most valuable effect and doubted if they could have produced such poise and maturity without it.

However, this appears to be one feature of LOGO which Papert did not foresee. In *Mindstorms* he expressed the hope that LOGO would allow children and teachers to work without a lesson plan or set curriculum, and to have a more collaborative relationship; novices and experts learning together. And indeed many teachers stressed the importance of being willing to learn with the children and even at times to be taught by them. Several said that LOGO had taught them how to stand back and allow children to wrestle with difficulties, intervening only when frustration threatened to become overwhelming.

But Papert's attitudes to schools as such seems, at best, to be sceptical. He wrote of a growing disillusionment in America with traditional education. Classrooms, he says, are artificial and inefficient learning environments, created because society could find no better way to pass on certain skills like writing, grammar or 'school math'. He seemed to be hoping that with enough computers schools might either change or wither away completely and LOGO as an agent for group development does not seem to have been much on his mind.

# LOGO in British schools

British teachers, while grateful for Papert's LOGO, do not seem to share his apparent lack of faith in the value of the classroom as a learning environment. Every teacher in the study had given considerable thought to the optimum number for groups working with floor or screen Turtles and with experience, the sizes of groups often changed. They all felt strongly that children should not work at a computer alone. The most effective learning resulted from interaction between the groups working together with LOGO.

It may be that the child-centred approach to learning is more firmly rooted in British classrooms than appears to be common in the United States and that the development of social skills is cherished even more highly than fostering the individual.

A number of teachers described something that they called a LOGO culture, which they believed established itself in the classroom and resulted in a particular style of learning. I have strong reservations about this in particular. It has, after all, long been the tradition in many British primary schools that children's learning should be based on their own experiences and interests wherever possible, without relying on lesson plans or set curricula. The management style of many classrooms is designed to encourage the development of initiative and self-reliance.

It is not uncommon for classrooms to be set up as workshops, where children are trained from the age of five to select, use and return equipment and materials in a business-like manner. Close observation and individual responses are encouraged right across the curriculum.

Teachers with this background, accustomed to the idea that children should take the initiative for their own learning, that how children learn to think and work is as important as what they study, are unlikely to find the philosophy of *Mindstorms* revolutionary, and might question the notion that computers can be the sole or even the main agent for promoting logical, orderly thought in young children.

I, for one, remain unconvinced that children can only learn to be so clear-minded, fearless and responsible as a result of programming with LOGO. As more than one teacher I saw remarked, science activities, writing plays, staging dance or drama productions, can all produce equally impressive examples of poised and articulate young people.

Nevertheless, it is clear from the work I saw that LOGO does fit easily into good, child-centred British primary practice. It provides an interactive form of computer work which encourages children to choose an idea or topic for investigation and which allows them to shape that idea into a form which can be communicated to others. In that respect it is as creative as working with words, clay, paint, LEGO or any other material available in a primary school.

I was struck by the way that the children building the Big Ben model at Delves, for instance, were able to describe to me in fluent detail all the stages they had had to go through and all the problems they had had to overcome in order to construct it. The actual LOGO program controlling the chimes had been the least of their problems, but there seemed to be some connection between their experiences as programmers and the clarity with which they held forth.

All the teachers I saw had good relationships with their pupils. Even in classrooms which were not particularly democratically run the atmosphere was affectionate and sensitive to the children's needs, but one suspects that good work emerges from such an environment whatever the tool at hand.

However, it is also apparent that in the hands of teachers confident enough to admit to ignorance, who are willing to learn with their classes or even to allow their pupils to take the initiative and teach them on occasion, LOGO can be a very effective part of classroom life and children can use it to produce work of which any teacher would be proud.

## Evaluating LOGO

What about more formal attempts to evaluate LOGO? Derek Radburn had some comments to make:

'We should treat the research into LOGO with as much caution as the claims which are made for it.

Research can be useful, but if it concentrates on aspects of LOGO which are easy to measure, such as the cognitive areas, then not only is there a danger that LOGO may come to be seen exclusively as part of the maths curriculum, and so become locked into a rigid structure, but its effect on other important areas of learning will be missed.

Papert's cognitive perceptions are sound, but what really underlines LOGO is a humanistic faith in individuals as agents in their own learning. The research has difficulty handling that view, and in concentrating on applications such as maths it can produce a lopsided impression of LOGO's potential.'

Teachers, Radburn thinks, as the people who know what their children do best, should stick with their own values in using LOGO. 'They must go into it trusting their own intuitions.'

## Inservice training

*But what about teachers who, though sufficiently intrigued to make a start, feel diffident because they have no training? Surely support for them should be provided?*

'The way inservice training in LOGO is being handled worries me. Crash courses in LOGO are like snow in April; short-lived and messy. If people are put under pressure to introduce LOGO quickly, mistakes will be made which may have the effect of bringing LOGO into disrepute, especially if the people called on to train teachers are not properly equipped to handle the training.

I am reminded of what happened with Nuffield Science, with which I was also involved. A lot of money was made available for a crash programme of training, but at the end of the day, though some excellent guides were produced, very little has happened in classrooms. I think this is because the material that was presented to the teachers was too generalised and based exclusively on what the children needed. Not enough thought was given to what the inexperienced teachers might need to get started.

LOGO could easily go the same way. If teachers are given some examples of very nice work going on in schools where people have had plenty of time to develop it, they may very well become intimidated into believing work of that quality is beyond them. And crash courses round the country involving a sketchy introduction to the philosophy and language won't lead to successful work in classrooms either.

What is important is the way that LOGO gets used by individual teachers in their own classrooms. Walsall LOGO has a basic soundness about it because it was developed in this way. I know several teachers who looked very unpromising to start with, but who have taken to LOGO with enthusiasm after having a chance to see teachers and children in their own schools using it and been able to see for themselves what the children were getting from it.

What we need is evolution of LOGO into education, not a revolution.'

## Hardware implications

*Even if appropriate backup and training are provided what are the hardware implications for schools?*

Many teachers in this study felt that if children were to have a chance of exploiting LOGO's potential fully then each school would need at least one machine dedicated to it full time. Most of these teachers wanted to be able to explore other aspects of computer work such as word processing, adventure games and data retrieval. If they had to limit themselves to only one aspect of computer work, they would, however reluctantly, concentrate on LOGO.

Several people pointed out the fact that a number of relatively cheap machines such as the Sinclair Spectrum, Commodore and particularly the Atari with its Sprites, have excellent LOGOs, so schools might be able to buy for themselves a machine which could be dedicated to LOGO, in addition to the standard government subsidised model.

I noticed that children seemed to have a remarkable capacity for coping with the slightly different versions of LOGO produced by the various machines. Some developed a preference for one over another and teachers thought it was beneficial for children to have access to several versions, just as some schools preferred to offer a range of reading schemes or mathematics books.

By working with several brands of LOGO on different microcomputers over the years, children could learn certain generalisations about how computers work, and could understand what the essential keys and functions were, regardless of where they were located on particular keyboards. Swapping from machine to machine also encouraged children to record their plans in computer notebooks and gave them time to reflect upon exactly what they were trying to achieve. Some children, however, were able to explore directly with a keyboard, regardless of the particular syntax of the LOGO they were using.

On the issue of full LOGO versus DART and ARROW both sides seem to have a point. Advocates of full LOGO point out that we talk to babies in adult language because we believe that they will eventually have a richer command of language if they hear it in its full complexity from the beginning. To these people restricting children to a subset of LOGO is analagous to teaching children to read in pictograms at first, instead of English, because it is easier. To start without a complete LOGO, they say, ignores the fact that it is powerful enough to be used in secondary schools and beyond. Whether secondary schools are preparing to deal with the young LOGO experts who will be coming to them soon is a fascinating question which falls outside my present brief.

But just as English, in Derek Radburn's words, is 'used equally by a three year old and a barrister for their own purpose at their own level' so LOGO is equally extensible and, therefore, it should be introduced immediately and in its full form. Yet I was also impressed with the argument that many teachers found programs like DART and ARROW a less intimidating starting point.

## Children in control

In any event, at the end of my brief journey through this new territory, I am left, above all, with an abiding impression of the enormous flexibility of young minds and the range of skills which they can deploy given the right opportunities.

I remember the anxiety with which we primary teachers faced decimalisation. Would children be able to deal with such small units as the centimetre and the rapid move to tens and hundreds that would result? But in the classrooms I visited for this Project, inches and feet are not even a memory. True, teachers have had to be skillful in helping six year olds cope with Turtle units involving 90s or 180s.

Most significantly of all, whether LOGO is revolutionary or simply a useful new tool, the children I observed were at home with computers. They believed themselves to be the masters of machines. In an age when computers could overwhelm the societies which invented them, that aspect of LOGO alone would be sufficient grounds for welcoming it into our schools.

*LOGO fits easily into a busy classroom.*

# SOME USEFUL RESOURCES

*Mathematics Counts — Report of the Committee of Inquiry into the Teaching of Mathematics in Schools* by W H Cockcroft (Her Majesty's Stationery Office, London, 1982).

*Teaching and Learning with LOGO* by Allan Martin (Croom Helm, Kent, 1986).
A thorough discussion of LOGO including imaginative uses of LOGO at school and at home.

*Microworlds Adventures with LOGO* by Richard Noss, Clare Smallman and Michael Thorne (Hutchinson, London, 1985).
Creative possibilities of microworlds: mini-environments for exploring ideas.

*LOGO: A Guide to Learning* by Peter Goodyear (Heinemann, London, 1984).
Very good overview of LOGO.

*Learning with Apple LOGO* by Daniel Watt (McGraw Hill, Maidenhead, 1983).
Practical book with helpful explanations for pupils.

*Let's Talk Apple Turtle* by Liddy Neville and Carolyn Dowling (Prentice-Hall, Hemel Hempstead, 1983).
Full of ideas for complementary activities away from the computer.

*On the Right Trak . . . with Big Trak* by Walsall LOGO Project (Walsall LEA, 1983).
Book for teachers with suggested activities for children.

*Children Learning LOGO* by Chiltern LOGO Project (Advisory Unit for Computer Based Education, Hatfield, 1983).
Contains examples of children's work with LOGO.

*Learning and Teaching with Computers* by Tim O'Shea and John Self (Harvester Press, Sussex, 1983)
Broader than LOGO and includes useful ideas.

*Posing and Solving Problems with LOGO* — a teacher training pack (MEP National Primary Project). Available from Northern Micro Media, Newcastle Polytechnic, Coach Lane Campus, Newcastle Upon Tyne NE7 7XA.
A comprehensive teacher training pack which includes tutor guidelines, articles, OHPs, a resources booklet and some programs.

*Posing and Solving Problems using Control Technology* — a teacher training pack (MEP National Primary Project). Available either from your LEA computer advisor or the National Primary Project, St James' Hall, King Alfred's College, Winchester, Hampshire SO22 4NR.
The pack includes a disk called *Controller,* which is a collection of computer files designed to extend a full LOGO into control applications.

*Turning Point* — a film about primary aged children using LOGO. Available from Videotext Educational Publishing, Orders Department, Eagle Star House, New North Road, Exeter EX4 4HF. Tel: 0392 219309. Price: £24.55 plus VAT and postage.

A video narrated by Beverly Anderson to accompany the teacher training pack *Posing and Solving Problems With LOGO* (MEP National Primary Project). The *Times Educational Supplement* (15.11.85) described it as '. . . gives ideas and the necessary motivation for those teachers interested in exploring the potential of LOGO more fully'.

*Seeing and Doing Computers* — teacher's notes to accompany five television programmes to be repeated on ITV in the spring term 1987. Available from The Schools Publication Officer, Thames Television, 149 Tottenham Court Road, London W1P 9LL. Price £1.20.

*Wondermaths — LOGO* (BBC Television for Schools) — five 15-minute programmes for upper primary children to start in spring term 1987. The material is suitable for total beginners though parts of it will be appropriate to those with moderate LOGO experience. Topics include Turtle graphics and other applications of LOGO. For further information contact School Broadcasting Information, The School Broadcasting Council, Villiers House, The Broadway, Ealing, London W5 2PA. Tel: 01-991 8015.

## Some addresses

**The British LOGO Users' Group**
c/o London New Technology Centre
86-100 St Pancras Way
London
NW1 9ES

**Chiltern LOGO Project**
Advisory Unit for Computer Based Education
Endymion Road
Hatfield
Hertfordshire
AL10 8AU

Contact: Katrina Blythe

**Walsall LOGO Project**
Busill Jones School
Ashley Road
Bloxwich
Walsall
West Midlands
WS3 2QF

Contact: Linda Spear

# APPENDIX

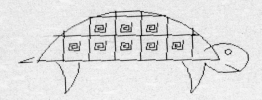

# TURTLE

```
?POTS                   ?POPS
TO FLIPBIT2
TO FLIPBIT               TO FLIPBIT2              TO GRID2
TO FLIPHALF2            FD 5                      BK 14
TO FLIPHALF            LT 3                      RT 90
TO FLIPPER2            END                       PD
TO FLIPPER                                        FD 13
TO GRID2                                          BK 282
TO CIRCLEBIT            TO FLIPBIT                PU
TO SEMICIRCLE          FD 5                      FD 67
TO SHIFT2             RT 3                      LT 90
TO SPIRAL             END                       FD 43
TO GRID                                           RT 90
TO SHIFT                                          PD
TO SHELL2              TO FLIPHALF2              FD 148
TO HEADTOP            REPEAT 15 [FLIPBIT2]       PU
TO HEADTOP2           END                       END
TO HEADTOP3
TO EYEBIT             TO FLIPHALF
TO HEADBIT2           REPEAT 15 [FLIPBIT]
TO TURTLE             END                        TO CIRCLEBIT
TO START                                         FD 17
TO HEADBIT            TO FLIPPER2                RT 5
TO TAIL               LT 52                      END
TO EYE                PU
TO SHELL              FD 200                     TO SEMICIRCLE
TO HEAD               LT 90                      REPEAT 26 [CIRCLEB
                       PD                         END
                       FLIPHALF
                       RT 142                     TO SHIFT2
                       FLIPHALF2                  PU
                       END                        LT 90
                                                  FD 25
                       TO FLIPPER                 RT 90
                       PD                         FD 60
                       RT 125                     RT 90
                       FLIPHALF                   FD 15
                       RT 142                     PD
                       FLIPHALF2                  END
                       END
```

```
TO SPIRAL
FD 20
RT 90
FD 20
RT 90
FD 15
RT 90
FD 15
RT 90
FD 10
RT 90
FD 10
RT 90
FD 5
RT 90
FD 5
END

TO GRID
RT 113
FD 353
PU
BK 50
RT 90
PD
FD 67
PU
BK 67
RT 90
FD 50
LT 90
PD
FD 97
PU
BK 97
RT 90
FD 50
LT 90
PD
FD 111
PU
BK 111
RT 90
FD 50
LT 90
PD
FD 109
PU
BK 109
RT 90
FD 50
LT 90
PD
FD 96
PU
BK 90
RT 90
FD 50
LT 90
PD
FD 64
PU
END
```

```
TO SHIFT
PU
LT 90
FD 25
LT 90
FD 40
LT 90
FD 15
PD
END

TO SHELL2
SPIRAL
SHIFT2
SPIRAL
SHIFT2
SPIRAL
SHIFT2
SPIRAL
PU
END

TO HEADTOP
REPEAT 16 [HEADBIT]
END

TO HEADTOP2
REPEAT 12 [HEADBIT2]
END

TO HEADTOP3
REPEAT 15 [HEADBIT]
END

TO EYEBIT
FD 2
RT 20
END

TO HEADBIT2
FD 5
RT 10
END

TO TURTLE
RT 30
SEMICIRCLE
GRID
GRID2
SHELL
SHELL2
HEAD
FLIPPER
FLIPPER2
TAIL
END

TO HEADBIT
FD 5
RT 5
END
```

```
TO TAIL
PU
LT 52
FD 47
PD
FD 25
RT 160
FD 30
PU
END

TO EYE
REPEAT 18 [EYEBIT]
END

TO SHELL
BK 15
RT 90
FD 15
PD
SPIRAL
SHIFT
SPIRAL
SHIFT
SPIRAL
PU
RT 90
FD 15
RT 90
FD 40
LT 90
FD 15
PD
SPIRAL
SHIFT2
END

TO HEAD
PU
RT 15
FD 53
LT 55
PD
HEADTOP
HEADTOP2
RT 50
FD 30
PU
BK 30
LT 50
PD
HEADTOP3
PU
RT 90
FD 50
PD
EYE
PU
BK 50
END
```

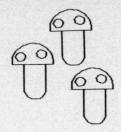

# TOADSTOOL

```
?POTS
TO SPOT
TO U
TO TOADSTOOL
TO D


?POPS
TO SPOT
REPEAT 20 [FD 2 RT 18]
END

TO U
PD
FD 37
REPEAT 22 [FD 2 LT 8]
LT 4
FD 40
PU
END

TO TOADSTOOL
U
LT 90
BK 10
D
RT 120
FD 20
PD
SPOT
PU
LT 40
FD 23
PD
SPOT
PU
END

TO D
PD
FD 53
RT 90
REPEAT 7 [FD 11 RT 24]
FD 11
RT 12
FD 6
PU
END
```

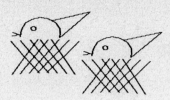

# BIRD

```
?POTS
TO NEST
TO TAIL
TO BEAK
TO BIRDSEYE
TO EYE
TO DBIT
TO XBIT
TO X
TO BIRD
TO BODY


?POPS
TO NEST
REPEAT 5 [XBIT]
END


TO TAIL
LT 140
PD
FD 55
LT 150
FD 50
PU
BK 50
LT 30
FD 55
RT 50
FD 53
END


TO BEAK
PD
LT 15
FD 10
PU
BK 10
RT 30
PD
FD 10
PU
BK 10
END
```

```
TO BIRDSEYE
RT 125
FD 20
PD
EYE
PU
END


TO EYE
REPEAT 20 [FD 1 RT 18]
END


TO DBIT
FD 11
RT 24
END


TO XBIT
X
LT 53
FD 25
RT 90
END


TO X
PD
RT 37
FD 62
PU
BK 31
LT 72
FD 31
PD
BK 62
PU
END


TO BIRD
NEST
BODY
TAIL
BEAK
BIRDSEYE
END
```

```
TO BODY
FD 50
LT 90
FD 53
RT 90
PD
REPEAT 7 [DBIT]
FD 7
RT 12
FD 6
PU
END
```

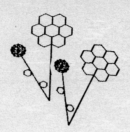

# FLOWER

```
?POTS
TO HEXAGON
TO HEADBIT
TO STALK
TO HEXAGON2
TO TWIG
TO BUD
TO FLOWER
TO HEAD


?POPS
TO HEXAGON
REPEAT 6 [FD 20 RT 60]
END

TO HEADBIT
HEXAGON
FD 20
LT 60
END

TO STALK
PU
LT 120
FD 20
LT 60
FD 20
PD
FD 170
RT 150
END

TO HEXAGON2
REPEAT 6 [FD 10 RT 60]
END

TO TWIG
FD 50
RT 30
HEXAGON2
LT 30
FD 50
LT 150
HEXAGON2
RT 150
FD 70
END
```

```
TO BUD
REPEAT 12 [HEXAGON2 LT 30]
END

TO FLOWER
HEAD
STALK
TWIG
BUD
END

TO HEAD
HEXAGON
LT 120
REPEAT 4 [HEADBIT]
HEXAGON
END
```

# RABBIT

```
?POTS
TO HEAD
TO BODY
TO EAR
TO WHISKERS
TO RABBIT


?POPS
TO HEAD
REPEAT 16 [FD 4 LT 5]
WHISKERS
REPEAT 15 [FD 4 LT 5]
RT 90
EAR
RT 135
REPEAT 13 [FD 4 LT 5]
RT 135
EAR
RT 90
REPEAT 15 [FD 4 LT 5]
WHISKERS
REPEAT 13 [FD 4 LT 5]
END

TO BODY
REPEAT 36 [FD 6 LT 5]
REPEAT 20 [FD 6 LT 18]
REPEAT 36 [FD 6 LT 5]
END

TO EAR
REPEAT 9 [FD 8 LT 5]
LT 135
REPEAT 9 [FD 8 LT 5]
END
```

```
TO WHISKERS
RT 105
FD 30
BK 30
LT 15
FD 30
BK 30
LT 15
FD 30
BK 30
LT 75
END

TO RABBIT
BODY
RT 180
HEAD
END
```

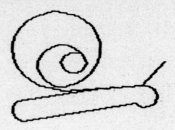

# SNAIL

```
?POTS
TO SHELL
TO SPIRALBIT6
TO CIRCLEBIT6
TO SPIRALBIT7
TO CIRCLEBIT7
TO SPIRALBIT8
TO CIRCLEBIT8
TO SPIRALBIT9
TO CIRCLEBIT9
TO SNAIL
TO BODY


?POPS
TO SHELL
SPIRALBIT9
SPIRALBIT8
SPIRALBIT7
SPIRALBIT6
END

TO SPIRALBIT6
REPEAT 6 [CIRCLEBIT6]
END

TO CIRCLEBIT6
FD 5
LT 8
END

TO SPIRALBIT7
REPEAT 30 [CIRCLEBIT7]
END

TO CIRCLEBIT7
FD 5
LT 10
END
```

```
TO SPIRALBIT8
REPEAT 15 [CIRCLEBIT8]
END

TO CIRCLEBIT8
FD 5
LT 18
END

TO SPIRALBIT9
REPEAT 8 [CIRCLEBIT9]
END

TO CIRCLEBIT9
FD 5
LT 36
END

TO SNAIL
SHELL
BODY
END

TO BODY
FD 50
LT 45
FD 25
BK 25
RT 45
REPEAT 6 [FD 5 RT 36]
FD 5
LT 43
FD 75
RT 36
REPEAT 4 [FD 5 RT 36]
FD 55
END
```